Balancing Connection

Lessons From AcroYoga That Lead to More Secure Relationships

Written by

Eric McKeethen

With Kate Burkett

Printed in the United States of America

First Edition, 2026

ISBN 979-8-9956105-1-9

Th'Architect Publishing
Dallas, TX
www.ThArchitect.net

Table of Contents

Acknowledgements vi
Glossary viii
Introduction 1
How to Use This Book 7
Part I 10
1. Acro and the Essence of Playfulness 13
Why a Book All About Acro Relationships? 13
The Wonder Induced by Acro 16
Background of AcroYoga in North America 19
Trust is Inherent in the Practice of Acro 21
How Acro Communities Build a Culture of Play 24
Navigating Challenges in the Acro Space 27
2. Playing Within Acro Relationships 31
Playfulness in Acro 33
Relationship Structure vs Emotional Experience 35
Emotional Attunement - Are Your Relationships FED? 40
Are You Beginning to Get Emotionally Close? 42
3. Developing Your Own Acro Relationships 46
Building Rapport and a Sense of Connection 47
Evaluating the Potential for Deeper Connection 50
Exploring the Idea of a New Partnership 52
Different Approaches to Relationships in Acro 55
Dealing with Fears and Feelings of Rejection 59
Part II 64
4. Brief Overview of Attachment Theory 69
Secure Attachment 72
When Attachment Needs Are Not Met 74

Insecure Attachment Styles ... 75
Viewing Attachment Needs as a Spectrum ... 86
5. Blending Attachment to Connection ... 93
Boundaries and the Giving and Receiving of Care ... 97
Healthy Boundaries ... 101
Porous Boundaries ... 103
Rigid Boundaries ... 105
Boundaries and Self-Identity/Self-Worth ... 107
6. Relationship Frameworks to Improve Communication ... 111
A Basis to Understand Relationship Success ... 113
Having curiosity about your partner ... 115
Sharing Fondness and Appreciation ... 118
Creating a Shared Reality ... 120
Being Responsive to Your Partner's Needs ... 122
Avoiding the Indicators of Unhealthy Relationships ... 127
7. The Nested Model of Attachment Experiences ... 131
Defining Trauma and Attachment Wounds ... 132
Self Level ... 135
Relationship Level ... 137
Home Level ... 139
Local Communities and Culture Level ... 141
Social Level ... 143
Global or Collective Level ... 146
Part III ... 152
8. The Foundations of Being AcroSecure ... 156
Do We Want to Be Attachment-Based Partners? ... 157
Communication and Shared Understanding ... 160
Understanding Boundaries and the Power of No ... 163
Develop an Openness to Connection ... 166

Expectations vs Agreements vs Rules 171
9. Broad Strokes of Being AcroSecure 178
Ways to Be There For Your Partner 181
Listening to Connect and Support 184
Roles You Can Serve in Your Relationships 188
10 The ACRO of Being AcroSecure 199
The A in ACRO: Attunement to Build Trust 201
The C in ACRO: Celebrate Astonishment 205
The R in ACRO: Rituals and Routines 208
The O in ACRO: Openness After Conflict 211
11. ACRO on Your Own: Secure Attachment with Self 216
Go ACRO On Your Own 218
A in ACRO: Attuning to Yourself 219
C in ACRO: Celebrate and Enjoy Your Thoughts 224
R in ACRO: Rituals and Routines for a Secure Self 226
O in ACRO: Be Open After Inner Conflict 229
12. Spotting Techniques For Being AcroSecure 234
Keeping Relationships Secure 235
Communicate Early and with Care 238
How Attachment Pairings Shape Relationship Dynamics .. 240
How to Approach Jealousy When it Arises 242
Compersion and Enjoying Other's Joy 244
Navigating Conflict and Friction Healthily 245
Relationship Renewal 249
13. Acro Relationships and Dealing with Past Trauma 252
Triggers and Dynamics Common in Acro Communities 254
How Acro Supports Healing in Attachment and Trauma ... 261
Bibliography 272
About the Authors 285

Acknowledgements

From Kate:

My Acro connection journey has been strongly shaped by my teacher Lux who taught me the value of using clear conscious communication in my partner acrobatics practice. A special thanks to my first and most bad ass acro partner Pat. I shout out to Chris who continues to inspire and motivate me on my acro journey. Lastly thank you for your wisdom Aunt Cathie, you are an editing Wizardess.

From Eric:

Nobody writes a book like this alone. That is just reality. Behind every finished manuscript is a supporting cast of people who taught you, challenged you, supported you, and occasionally shoved you toward the thing you were clearly supposed to do.

First, my mom. She showed me, by example, how to treat people well and how to genuinely connect with them. Not in a performative, "look how nice I am" way, but in the real way that actually matters when life gets messy and people need care, respect, and presence. A lot of what's good in me started there.

The Yoga Movement deserves real gratitude for giving me an empowering place to learn AcroYoga and find community. Good communities do more than teach skills. They give people a place to belong, to grow, and to become more of themselves. That place did that for me.

Austin from Austin gets a huge thank-you for introducing me to AcroYoga in the first place. That introduction lit the fuse. What started as a spark became a full-on fire, and a big part of my life has grown out of that one moment.

Nick from the AcroVan, thank you for showing me standing Acro. That was one of those moments where your brain quietly says, "Oh, so we're doing this now," and suddenly the whole horizon gets bigger.

Pitch Catch Circus School absolutely supercharged my learning journey. Some places help you improve. Others launch you. Pitch Catch did the latter. The training, the people, and the culture pushed my growth in ways I'm still benefiting from.

To the authors and researchers whose work I sourced in this book: thank you for doing the hard intellectual labor of creating useful material instead of empty noise. A lot of what's valuable in these pages stands on foundations you helped build.

And finally, my wife, Marissa. Thank you for your support and your adventurousness. Writing a book is one thing. Building a life with someone who is willing to keep saying yes to growth, risk, exploration, and all the uncertainty that comes with them, that's a gift. You've been that gift to me. I'm deeply grateful.

Books may have an author's name on the cover, but they are always built by a community. This one was too.

Glossary

Absorbing*: A porous-boundary pattern in which you take in other people's emotions, judgments, or needs so strongly that your own inner clarity gets overridden.*

Accurate self-assessment*: The ability to honestly judge your current physical, emotional, and mental readiness, especially before taking risks or making commitments.*

Acrobatic skill / skill: *A learned acro movement, shape, or sequence practiced with technique, repetition, and coordination.*

Agency*: The drive to act from your own will, make choices, and maintain a sense of autonomy.*

Aligned self*: The version of you that acts in line with your values, needs, intentions, and deeper truth rather than fear, pressure, or old survival patterns.*

Attachment wounds*: Lasting relational hurts that disrupt a person's ability to trust, give, or receive love safely, often because important attachment needs were not met or were violated.*

Aversion to touch*: A strong discomfort with physical contact, often shaped by past experience, trauma, sensory sensitivity, or learned fear.*

Avoidance: *Saying no to good things such as support, closeness, or help because vulnerability feels risky.*

Bid for affection: *A small verbal, emotional, or physical reach for closeness, attention, or care from another person.*

Blocking: *A rigid-boundary pattern in which you shut out feedback, care, influence, or emotional input from others in order to stay protected.*

Climate-related trauma: *Grief, fear, helplessness, or destabilization linked to climate change, environmental degradation, or climate disasters.*

Collective trauma: *Trauma experienced not only by individuals but by whole groups, communities, or societies.*

Communion: *The drive for closeness, belonging, acceptance, and emotional connection with others.*

Compersion: *Joy in another person's joy, especially when someone you care about experiences happiness, connection, or success.*

Compliance: *A boundary difficulty in which you say yes when you really mean no, often to avoid conflict or disapproval.*

Continuity of connection: *The felt trust that a bond remains real and meaningful through time apart, stress, or conflict.*

Controlling: *A boundary problem in which a person tries to override, manage, or challenge another person's limits rather than respecting them.*

Dopamine: *A neurotransmitter involved in motivation, reward, and the sense of satisfaction that can follow effort, novelty, or success.*

Friendships of convenience: *Relationships that thrive in a shared setting without necessarily extending into deeper or more intentional connection outside that context.*

Intruding: *A porous-boundary pattern in which you cross too much into another person's space, emotions, or decisions.*

Oxytocin: *A hormone and neurotransmitter involved in bonding, social attachment, and aspects of stress regulation.*

Porous boundaries: *A boundary pattern in which a person stays open to others but not well protected. It can look like overextending, absorbing others' emotions, or saying yes when you mean no.*

Positive perspective: *A relational stance in which people are more likely to interpret one another with generosity, goodwill, and trust rather than negativity.*

Relational instability: *A state in which trust, safety, and constructive connection are weakened, making a relationship more vulnerable to erosion, chronic conflict, or breakdown.*

Relational object constancy: *The ability to trust that your connection and bond with someone will persist beyond an initial separation or conflict.*

Relationship depreciation: *Intentionally letting a relationship become less central, less frequent, or less invested.*

Relationship escalation: *Intentionally deepening a relationship through greater time, care, priority, vulnerability, or mutual investment.*

Relationship fortification: *Strengthening and maintaining an existing relationship in its current form.*

Relationship renewal: *The intentional process of updating a relationship as people grow and change. It involves checking in, reassessing needs, and adjusting the relationship to fit the present.*

Restraining: *A rigid-boundary pattern in which you hold back your feelings, preferences, affection, or voice so strongly that genuine expression and connection get cut off.*

Rigid boundaries: *A boundary pattern in which self-protection becomes so strong that it limits vulnerability, trust, and closeness. It can look like shutting people out, blocking support, or holding back feelings.*

Safe haven: *An attachment figure or relationship that offers comfort, reassurance, and emotional refuge when you are distressed.*

Secure base: *A stable source of safety and support from which a person can explore, take risks, and engage the world, knowing they can return to connection when needed.*

Self-agency perspective: *A boundary framework in which the focus is on what you will do to uphold your limits, rather than trying to control the other person.*

Spotter / Spotting: *In Acro, a* ***spotter*** *helps keep people physically and emotionally safe during practice.* ***Spotting*** *is the act of staying present and ready to add stability, or help someone land safely.*

Structural violence: *Harm caused by social, political, economic, or institutional arrangements that systematically block people from meeting basic needs or living with dignity and safety.*

Trauma: *An overwhelming experience, or series of experiences, that leaves lasting physical, emotional, psychological, relational, or spiritual impact.*

***Trigger management**: The practice of recognizing when you have been emotionally activated and choosing grounded, responsible actions rather than reacting automatically.*

Introduction

When I began working on this book in 2023, I had to move through many hesitations within myself. At the same time, I felt a deep urgency to begin. I was convinced that this work mattered, but doubt held me back. These were shaped by my own experiences in the world. After more than a decade of play in Acro, I have gained such powerful lessons that helped me move through those fears. Writing this book strengthened my belief that these lessons should not remain limited to small group settings. They deserved to be shared with anyone longing for more depth, more compassion, and more meaningful connection in their lives.

By the time I began this project, it had become increasingly clear to me that many of us were struggling to find this depth. Even before the global pandemic of 2020, the United States and much of the Western World were already in the midst of a loneliness crisis. People felt disconnected. More and more people were living without enough meaningful relationships or dependable support. At the same time, rates of depression and anxiety were rising, along with struggles related to mental clarity, emotional well-being, and early death.

When people do not feel supported, it changes the way they move through life. Many began to live from a mindset of scarcity. They were focused on holding on and trying not to lose even more. Disconnection becomes a painful cycle, affecting not only the individual, but also the wider web of relationships and communities around them.

Other powerful forces were also reshaping how we related to one another. The growth of the Internet and social media changed how we formed social circles and how we defined our communities. For some, this created access to belonging. They found support among people with shared interests, even across long distances. For others, it opened the door to unrealistic comparison and shallow relationships that could not truly reciprocate the energy they seemed to demand. Over time, these changes created a growing divide in personal experience, making it harder for people living in the same neighborhoods to understand and relate to one another.

I saw these patterns unfold around me. Some of my childhood friends seemed to fall deeper into isolation, with few opportunities to interrupt the cycle. Yet I also saw those who were emotionally thriving in the very same climate. That contrast stayed with me. The people who were doing well seemed to share certain patterns, and many of those patterns mirrored the values and behaviors I had witnessed in Acro communities.

One of the most powerful things I noticed in Acro communities was the way people created depth and meaning from even brief interactions, without needing those moments to last forever. It was a safe place for people to have spontaneous conversations with strangers. Platonic touch was welcomed and normalized. When fear, self-doubt, or uncertainty surfaced, there were often people nearby who responded with support. In a time when many forms of community were becoming thinner and more fragmented, spaces like Acro offered a meaningful sense of belonging, presence, and care. This reflects something many people describe when they look back on a fulfilled life; it is often the quality of connection, not just its duration, that matters most.

In my adult years, I have felt a deep calling to help people find more meaningful connection in their lives. I have discussed this sense of connection with many people in the Acro community who wanted resources to help guide important conversations and improve communication in both their acro partnerships and their other relationships. Again and again, I heard the same need: people wanted help building stronger, healthier, and more intentional bonds.

When I look back on the experiences that inspired my growth and kept me devoted to this practice, most of the lessons that shaped me came through other people. They came from those who supported me as I stretched beyond my comfort zone. They came from people who challenged me with care and those who helped me see new possibilities in myself and others. This book is one way of honoring that support. It is also my way of sharing what I have learned and offering a reminder to keep gratitude at the center of how we connect.

When I reflect on my own journey in Acro, I can see how many of the lessons I learned there have directly shaped the course of my life and prepared me to embrace healthier, more secure relationships. I did not come up with most of these ideas on my own, but I have been fortunate to learn from accomplished teachers, respected leaders, and the many incredible acrobats who have shared their wisdom with me along the way.

Through these experiences, I learned many things. I learned not to place people in fixed roles based only on my personal perspective. Instead, I now leave room for them to surprise me. Before AcroYoga, I was unfamiliar with platonic touch. I was astonished that healthy, abundant touch had a profound effect on my stress levels and mental clarity. These are only a few of the lessons that deeply changed me. I know that the Acro community has changed others, too. I have watched as many practitioners learned life-changing lessons of their own through this practice.

The lessons of AcroYoga stand out even more to me because I have seen them embraced not only across the United States, but around the world. I have had the opportunity to travel and teach AcroYoga in many different countries. What I have come to admire most is how consistently certain values appear across the globe in these communities. Each city has its own culture and its own approach to the practice, yet the same beneficial principles continue to appear again and again. There is a safety-first mindset, proactive communication, mutual care, and a spirit of playfulness at any age. Through my teaching and coaching, I made a point of carrying the best lessons from one community into the next. After gathering so much wisdom from Acro communities around the world, I now have the privilege of sharing some of the most meaningful lessons with you in these pages.

At the heart of all of this is a simple truth: when we embrace the relationships in our lives, we open ourselves to more fulfillment and a larger appreciation of the time we share with others. When we feel satisfied, it's easier to appreciate our differences rather than fear them. That openness gives people space to show up more fully as themselves. We stop needing them to confine themselves to the roles we expect them to play. Each person has unique gifts to offer, and when we are open to receiving those gifts, we honor what they give us and make the relationship more meaningful for everyone involved. When we stop limiting one another to only the roles we need, we create more room for generosity, abundance, and deeper forms of connection.

This book is intended to help readers better understand the organic and exciting experience of being part of an Acro community, but its lessons are not limited to Acro. This book offers anyone who wants meaningful connections a guide for turning that desire into deeper understanding and intentional action. Whether you apply these principles within the Acro community, or in other relationships and communities throughout your life, they can help you create bonds that are more supportive, fulfilling, and aligned with who you are. Your relationships only hold the meaning you choose to give them, so it is worthwhile to build relationships that truly matter to you. And while healthy relationships with others are important, so is your relationship with yourself. These same principles can also help you care for, strengthen, and soothe your connection with yourself.

So what can you gain from this book, or from experiences within an Acro community? Meaningful relationships can make you more resilient in the face of a changing world. They not only offer support during difficult times, but also create space for greater openness, trust, and possibility. Secure relationships can help you move through life with less fear and reactivity. They allow you to act with more intention and create deeper meaning from your efforts. Your sense of community does not have to be limited to one place or one group. You can belong to many communities at the same time, and each one can offer something valuable. The lessons in this book can help you become more intentional about how you engage, when you step back, and how you choose to show up.

If you are ready to take greater ownership of your relationships, this book is here to support you. That ownership is not about controlling how another person behaves. It is about becoming more intentional with how you show up in each moment. It's about deciding who you want to be in your relationships. You can learn to show up more fully and create the kind of space where deeper connection can grow. There is something within you that is ready to be expressed, and these lessons are here to help you bring it forward. Let this book guide you toward building relationships that call you forward and support the person you are becoming.

Personally, I'm proud of what this work has grown into. One of the mottos I live by is, "Be the light you want to see in the world." In both Acro partnerships and personal relationships, we are each called to set the example for how we want to be treated. We're each responsible for modeling what we hope to cultivate in our relationships and communities. The journey begins with the standard we're willing to set. I want to see the world around me shine, and I hope this work becomes one more way to help that light grow a little brighter.

"Surprise!"

–Eric McKeethen

How to Use This Book

We wrote this book as an actionable guide for you to take for yourself and your relationships today. We understand that each person learns and assimilates information differently, and we have included several ways that you can digest and use the content in this book to find the most effective means for you. We have included so much good content and information that you will be able to return to it on multiple occasions during your Acro journey, and even your lifetime-relationship journey, but we don't expect you to internalize all the concepts in the book at one time. There may be an individual issue you are facing immediately, so we have included some questions in each chapter that you may already be asking yourself or your partner. You can use these for exercises and actionable information.

The structure of the book is designed to walk you through an introduction to partner acro (AcroYoga) and the relationship dynamics that are common in the practice. This introduction shows some of the intersectionality that may be inherent to both partner acro and other kinds of partner practices, and where you can apply the principles and concepts in this book to those relationships. We elaborate on how attachment theory can be readily applied to relationship dynamics in the practice and the importance of bringing a conscious awareness of that connection to how we treat each other.

In the second part of the book, we dive deeper into attachment theory and how it explains the impacts of relationships on ourselves and vice versa. This helps bring light to some of the factors we may not be aware are making a daily impact on each of our interactions. In this part of the book, we also explore relationship frameworks developed by respected clinicians and grounded in research. Taking time to reflect on your own relationship history is a powerful way to take control of whether you want more or less of what you have been getting from relationships in your life.

For the third part of this book, we map out our guide to becoming AcroSecure and embracing the partnerships in your life to make them more rewarding. While we outline the principles of being AcroSecure in your relationships first, it really does begin with becoming AcroSecure within yourself, so we dedicate a whole chapter to this process. The transformation of yourself and your partnerships does not happen in a vacuum, so we also elaborate on how to address changes in relationship dynamics, along with common questions we have heard around these topics.

This will be a rewarding, but oftentimes challenging, journey to embrace secure partnerships in your life. We have laid out a great collection of information to serve as guideposts for you along this journey. This book should be revisited many times as both you and your relationships grow and change. We believe different concepts will become relevant for the different stages of your personal relationships. The main concepts, those listed in the Glossary, are highlighted in bold print.

We recognize that this book should not be your only resource as you embark on this journey and have shared many additional resources and books that we recommend in the Bibliography. Please jump around in this book as you find your own way. We wish you wonderful growth in your relationships and your life!

Part I

To start off this first part of the book, we offer a glimpse into the activity and community of partner acrobatics, also referred to as Acro. While each person may have different experiences within Acro, there are many aspects that bring all of us together. Both of us have had relatively long journeys within the community, with many of the experiences that most practitioners go through. Some of the experiences that stand out more vividly for us, and that we hear about often from others in the community, are hitting a skill for the very first time, and then having to struggle to hit the same skill a second time; receiving encouragement from others to try a skill that we thought was outside our reach; conversations that happen after everyone is worn out from a workout; and getting to teach a new skill to someone and seeing their expressions of accomplishment.

We have enjoyed practicing Acro and also sharing Acro with others.

There are so many different experiences within Acro, but there are several aspects that bring all of us together in community. Becoming a part of the community has been a very special experience for both of us. We will be sharing the things we know that help individuals become accustomed to the wider community and build better awareness of the individual communities we each step into. Getting into the community can be a simple endeavor, typically being shared from person to person.

We both got started in AcroYoga group classes and had teachers excited to share the skills and philosophy behind the practice. We were lucky to start in communities in larger cities, where there was a substantial group of people to connect with, allowing many people to cycle through the community without it collapsing.

There are a variety of people and backgrounds coming into the practice of AcroYoga. While it can be simple to join and practice Acro with others, sometimes it may not be as simple to understand the emotions behind the bodies we interact with. We have learned many lessons through our wide-ranging Acro journeys and feel fortunate to have been able to share these lessons with other community members and the acrobats we have coached. We know that there can be many struggles forming an Acro partnership, so we are starting this book by sharing some common background of the community, signs that show a deepening of relationships within Acro, and principles for deciding what kinds of relationships you want to develop through Acro.

The journey within Acro does not have to be complex, and in fact, much of it is simpler than you might expect. Going into your practice prepared for both the skills and interpersonal interactions will allow you to get even more out of your experiences. The desire within the community for all of us to help improve ourselves and each other is widespread and giving a common understanding of how we can treat each other is one of the goals we want to share through this work. As we have worked on this project, we have received abundant feedback that a book like this is needed. We see the impact that it can have and the impact that you can have in affecting the community you are in, as well as the wider community.

1

Acro and the Essence of Playfulness

Why a Book All About Acro Relationships?

From the outside, Acro can look like a daring experience. On the surface, it is a group of people working together to defy gravity. However, the practice of partner Acro is almost entirely about connection and playfulness. The ability to stack people on top of each other emerges from "let's see what happens when we…" just as much as it does from formal technique. From the basic movements of being suspended in the air during the "bird" or "child's plane" pose, where someone helps lift us into each position, we learn how to lean on another person in ways that we haven't outside of these partner practices. In this generation, leaning on and depending on another person may not be something that people are widely accustomed to. We all bring our own experiences into the practice and into our interactions with each other. Even the element of communication may not be common between practitioners. Each of us always has something that we can learn from the practice whether in shared spaces or on our own. Seeing people connect through this practice is rewarding and encourages us to want to better ourselves for our own sakes, in addition to wanting to better the communities we are a part of.

The Acro community has been expanding rapidly in North America since its introduction in 2003. While it has developed through the efforts of many dedicated teachers, it has grown primarily by being shared organically through the enthusiasm of people practicing in public spaces, including the Internet, and through the excitement of people seeing the practice. One of the more contagious aspects of Acro is the playfulness that it encourages. When we try skills in Acro, there is an embracing of enjoyment and a suspension of disbelief. We each get to do something that we wouldn't do in our normal lives and expand what we thought was possible. From the moment we do our first bird pose, to when we go upside down and stacked on another person, the constraints of what is normal continue to also be turned upside down. This playfulness is contagious and brings people together to form communities that support each other. It encourages rapid growth, both in skills and in relationships. We have seen how bringing this playfulness and enthusiasm into our lives and communities can create more fulfillment and connection.

Similar to when each of us played house or other make-believe scenarios as children, our time in Acro spaces creates a microcosm of the kinds of relationships we experience in other areas of our lives. A benefit of these relationships playing out in Acro is that it tends to happen in safer spaces, where there are other people to witness and share the experience. There are also teachers and spotters in most spaces. Even though there may be higher physical risks while practicing, there is also security in the emotional experience where safety spotters are available and more experienced teachers can provide in-the-moment feedback. The experiences we have with others within Acro can significantly influence how we understand relationships outside Acro spaces. While the norms of Acro communities establish themselves organically, the structure of Acro practice has been developed through intentional movements and organizations since the beginning of the millennium.

Having more materials and organizations that support a shared understanding within our communities can strengthen the culture of Acro in meaningful ways. When people have access to common language, relational frameworks, and guidance around communication, consent, boundaries, and care, it becomes easier for both leaders and community members to navigate challenges with more clarity and confidence. This can reduce some of the burden placed on teachers, organizers, and more experienced practitioners to constantly explain or mediate community dynamics in the moment. It can also help newer members feel more supported in understanding not only the physical practice, but also the relational culture that makes the practice safer, more welcoming, and more sustainable. Just as important, these understandings do not need to remain limited to Acro spaces. The skills people develop around communication, trust, self-awareness, and mutual care carry over into friendships, families, romantic relationships, and other communities. Over time, these kinds of resources can help smooth interactions, deepen trust, and create communities that are better equipped to grow with intention rather than relying only on informal trial and error. In other words, this growth applies not only within Acro communities, but also in the broader relational lives of the people who move through them.

The Wonder Induced by Acro

Each of us has experienced moments that sparked sheer amazement and boundless imagination. Maybe it was while sitting in a darkened theater, eyes wide with wonder, watching as a superhero soared effortlessly through the sky, cape billowing behind them, or swung gracefully from towering skyscraper to skyscraper with breathtaking speed. Or perhaps it was witnessing an elite athlete in the heat of competition, defying gravity with a high-flying flip, landing with perfect balance and control, as the crowd erupts in awe. Or maybe it happened under the spotlight on a grand stage, where a circus performer balanced precariously high above the ground, executing a heart-stopping, death-defying stunt with elegance and precision, leaving you breathless and on the edge of your seat. While these examples may seem out of reach for most of us to visualize ourselves doing on our own, seeing a person in the park less than 10 meters away suspended in the air, brings on much of the same wonder. Seeing this kind of moment so close in our own lives can feel more approachable than those larger-than-life stages. Where this wonder meets curiosity creates the possibility for perspective-altering experiences when one of these "people in the park" calls out to a bystander to join, and that bystander happens to say yes…

> *"I was introduced to AcroYoga very randomly while being a date at a sorority formal event in Austin, TX. I was talking with another one of the dates at the event when he mentioned that he taught AcroYoga. I asked him, 'What is AcroYoga?,' and he asked me if I would like him to show me. When I said yes, he grabbed my hands and fell backward onto the dance floor and put me on his feet. I am a pretty large man, and he was able to keep me suspended off the ground and guide me through different positions. I pretty much have not felt that manipulated and lightweight since I was a young child. The way that I felt in that moment was first disbelief, and then amazement and fascination that this was actually happening, and finally a hunger to do this again. After being placed back on the ground, I thanked him enthusiastically and wondered where I could learn how to do more of this. When I returned to Dallas, I looked up classes in town. After going to my first class, I didn't miss a week of Acro for 4 years." —Eric McKeethen, co-author of this book*

These moments were life-altering and impactful for both of us authors and led us down journeys that we are amazed and grateful for. We are sharing our learnings from our journey with Acro, and best practices from the wider community, because we were changed by these spontaneous occurrences.

> *"My whole life I loved team or partnered sports and anything that felt a little risky. While living in Hawai'i I had tried tandem surfing and loved the feeling of being lifted*

over my partner's head while catching a wave. As a yoga teacher I was always open to new kinds of movement practices. A girlfriend of mine in Seattle asked me if I had ever tried AcroYoga. I hadn't and I was not even sure what she was talking about. This was in 2013, before viral Instagram AcroYoga accounts were a thing. She took me to a casual private AcroYoga event in someone's home. The first time being lifted up, stretched, and twirled around by another human was nothing short of life changing. I left that event feeling exhilarated. I was literally obsessed with AcroYoga. I couldn't stop thinking about it. I started going to every Acro meetup and class I could find. The rest is history, AcroYoga has been my passion ever since. I love the journey of continued learning, I love teaching, and I can't seem to get enough of this dynamic partner practice!" — Kate Burkett, co-author of this book

The shared environment created in Acro opens a space for our imagination to roam and gives us the safety to explore daring ideas. A common statement that we have heard at the beginning of a class or session is, "Wow! I could never do that." There may be so much doubt around a new student's role in these skills, yet when they allow themselves to be open to trying something with a playful mindset and with the group, they frequently find themselves doing movements they never imagined themselves doing. Having fun and releasing the expectations of certain outcomes provides room for wonder to emerge within them. One person in the group can see the possibility and guide the rest of the group to accomplishing it, even when it may be beyond their individual perceived limits. The encouragement and safety structures that are available while doing Acro can lead us to push beyond what we thought we were capable of doing. This magical process of achieving feats outside our own conceptions and sharing that with others is part of the wonder that keeps each of us coming back to Acro.

Background of AcroYoga in North America

AcroYoga is a practice that blends acrobatics with yoga and Thai massage. It can also include elements from cheerleading, circus acrobatics, and other bodywork modalities. The skills in AcroYoga are done as partner- or group-exercises. There are many different styles of AcroYoga depending on where in the world you are and what community you are a part of. For the purposes of this book, we will focus on the background of AcroYoga as it has developed in North America.[1]

The common practice of Acro has primarily been developed and become widespread due to the influence of two organizations: AcroYoga Montreal in Canada and AcroYoga Inc. in California. Both have made names for themselves in acrobatic yoga. They began teaching and sharing the practice around a similar time.

Acroyoga Montreal, AYM, was established in 1999 and fully realized its methodology in 2003. The style of the founders, Eugene Poku and Jessie Goldberg, blends dance, yoga, and acrobatics, and supports that blend of active movement with restorative and yin yoga. Later, their style became known as "Acroyoga Fusion." Also in 2003, AcroYoga International was established in California. Founded by Jason Nemer and Jenny Sauer-Klein, this methodology is focused around solar practices, based on sports acrobatics and vinyasa yoga, and lunar practices, based on Thai massage. For many years after 2003, "Acroyoga" was a trademarked term and only certified teachers who had studied and been certified by Nemer and Sauer-Klein were allowed to use it. The term has been made available for use to the wider community since then. Both organizations have helped bring AcroYoga into the consciousness of the much broader culture.

While the structure of Acro, as it is commonly known, has only been around since 2003, the basics of the practice, the skills and techniques, can be traced back much further. Many of the active skills and techniques can be tied back to circus and partner acrobatics. While some of the earliest accounts of acrobatics, from as far back as 2000 BCE, describe performances in China during the Xia and Shang dynasties, partner acrobatics was more reliably accounted for in 18th century European circuses. It was known then as "hand-to-hand" or "adagio" acts, often highlighting strength, balance, and trust between performers. Partner acrobatics, as a sport, flourished in the Soviet Union in the 1900s, and in 1939 they wrote the first rules for this new sport to hold a national championship. Later on, acrobatic gymnastics evolved in other European countries. In 1957, the first "International Acro Tournament" was held, featuring athletes from the Soviet Union, German Democratic Republic, Poland, and Bulgaria.

Many of the restorative practices can be tied back to the teachings of Krishnamacharya. The Indian yoga teacher established many techniques contributing to modern yoga. He also developed many of the exercises used in Thai massage as early as 1938. For him, the focus was on "therapeutic flying" and using the body to suspend another for healing.

Each community's leaders bring their own expertise to their teachings. Whether they have taken a certification course from one of the teaching organizations or learned their techniques from a mentor, there are common basics that form a foundation for the practices in North America. There may be different terminology and progressive steps depending on the community and geographic area, but when you are able to break them down, you can take the skills to any other community and find a common understanding of how to communicate and play.

Trust is Inherent in the Practice of Acro

There are so many aspects in the playful practice of Acro that lend themselves to a more fulfilling life experience and personal growth. The quick feedback loop of trial and error to success allows each of us to learn how to face setbacks. Breaking through those setbacks creates so many moments of joy in finding success in the movements. Dealing with each of these setbacks and successes creates a bountiful environment for trust to develop. Not only is trust developed between partners, but a significant amount of trust also has to be developed with the other people in a training space and the community as a whole. As stated by Simon Sinek,[2] "We don't build trust by offering help, we build trust by asking for it." Learning to be open to help, and asking for it, is a skill in itself. Being able to rely on your partner to do their part in the skill and to avoid hurting you is supported by the actions of a Spotter in the situation. Having consistent events and spaces in which to practice lends to a valuable sense of being a part of the community.

When you get to see acrobats in action, you can observe the intentional synergy of their actions working together to create shapes and movements. It is necessary to work with another person in Acro because of the different roles that support each other. The person who is being lifted off the ground is called the Flyer. They are most often responsible for changing and holding positions with their body. Whereas, the person who is lifting and holding the other person off the ground is called the Base, and is most often responsible for providing a stable connection from the Flyer to the ground. In practice and supportive situations, a Spotter plays a pivotal role in maintaining the physical and mental safety of everyone involved. While the Spotter may not be physically touching the Base or Flyer during the movements, they provide a sense of safety and encouragement. When a movement becomes out of control, the Spotter adds stability or prioritizes bringing the Flyer toward the ground safely and preventing injury for both the Flyer and Base. Additionally when there are three or more people physically involved in the skill, the Mid is a role that is not always involved, but takes the actions of both Flyer and Base within a sequence or routine. When these roles work together and there is trust in each other to do their parts, the astounding movements within Acro become possible and rewarding.

One of the fundamental principles in Acro, taught early on, is to focus on pushing into your partner during movements rather than pulling against them. When adjusting or trying to find the right position, it is more effective to press into the points of connection you share with the other person, instead of pulling on parts of their body. Although there are occasional moments in Acro when pulling may be necessary, these are much rarer. This principle helps reduce shakiness and improves the predictability of movement. When you're focused on pushing, you naturally start to pay attention to where and how much pressure you're applying, making it easier for your partner to respond to and anticipate your movements. As you reach out, it becomes clear that there's a limit to how far from yourself you can extend while still pushing effectively.

This concept offers a powerful metaphor for AcroSecure relationships. If we think of pushing as "giving," we learn to lead with the energy we want in relationships, rather than centering on what we're receiving. At the same time, we must also be aware of how much we can give in a healthy way, which informs our boundaries. In order to receive the pressure or support our partner is offering, we must also learn to be stable.

Another core principle in Acro is developing stability. We need to build the capacity to remain grounded and steady, even in unpredictable situations. This includes minimizing the risk of losing control over our limbs or allowing them to buckle, which in turn strengthens the confidence and trust in our connection points.

Metaphorically, this reflects the importance of personal stability in relationships. Through healthy boundaries and self-awareness, we become more resilient and responsive. As we build consistency in how we show up and react, our partners are better able to trust our actions and commitments.

Diving into how to have a healthy and secure relationship with an Acro partner will allow a strong and fulfilling Acro practice to develop, but also will give space within those relationships to feel safe and supported emotionally as well as physically. The things that come up while practicing within an Acro partnership, are almost always symptoms of what is happening in the relationship with that person outside of practice. The practice of Acro just puts a microscope on the issues or strengths that exist within the relationship. Romantic couples who start doing Acro together show many of the communication habits they each have, but in a more condensed space. Couples where one partner often speaks over the other will very likely have the more outspoken partner giving more instructions and feedback to the other. This can create an imbalance in the Acro partnership and does not allow for healthy growth for both people. Similarly, when one partner often dismisses the feelings of the other, they will typically take less feedback from their partner while practicing Acro and be less responsive to making changes to accommodate for their partner's comfort.

How Acro Communities Build a Culture of Play

Acro communities have taught and encouraged several

values that enable a culture of playfulness to flourish. Practicing Acro typically has to be done in groups, and this leads to organic communities, often based on geographic areas. Within each of these communities there are norms and rules. Navigating the interactions of each class or event can serve as a reflection of how we each deal with cooperation and conflict, along with inner fears and insecurities. Proactive communication, consent, emotional safety, and physical safety provide important pillars in creating a playful environment. These same principles are also important in developing healthy, secure bonds, which we will explore in later chapters. For now, we will expand on how these values show up in the Acro community.

With higher levels of potential risk in practicing Acro, proactive communication between everyone involved is emphasized in order to bring awareness about what may happen and how to keep everyone safe. When trying a skill with someone, a conversation about each person's intentions and expectations will get everyone on the same page. These conversations are encouraged to happen beforehand because people have many different backgrounds and understandings of how movements are supposed to progress. Misunderstandings in the middle of a movement can be dangerous. While proactive communication is valued across all Acro communities, the specifics of what is discussed beforehand differ from community to community. It is important while practicing that you proactively bring up any concern that ensures your own safety and comfort.

The element of consent is taught early and reinforced often

in most intro Acro classes. Asking for consent before touching another person's body is very important in creating a safe space where each person can feel comfortable having others enter their personal space, especially when touching someone's hips or shoulders. These discussions include asking for consent before engaging in movement. Additionally, there are often check-ins to ensure that everyone involved still feels comfortable with what has been happening and what will be coming up next. Each person may have different needs that should be considered before taking action. Within the Acro community, we err toward establishing consent more often than not. We will not cover all of the intricacies of consent here, but some aspects that we will cover in-depth later in this book are the dimensions of explicit or implicit consent; verbal or nonverbal consent; and enthusiastic or reluctant consent. Outside of consent about physical interactions, the consent to give or receive feedback and unsolicited critiques should be established early on in an interaction. This is also an important contribution to safety and comfort within the community.

Safety in Acro is one of the most widely discussed topics, from within individual communities to the wider Acro community. Since Acro has increasingly riskier consequences as the complexity of the movements increase, there are discussions at each event and class on how to approach the practice in ways that minimize bad consequences. Because there are many in-depth discussions and guidelines about safety that go hand in hand with the sharing of advanced skills, the practice of AcroYoga has been able to grow and expand quickly over the past decade in the United States. Since the onset, there has always been an emphasis on physical safety in Acro, but in more recent years there has also been a large push to improve the emotional safety of people practicing Acro.

Navigating Challenges in the Acro Space

There are many values that help people grow within the Acro community. But we also want to share some of the concerns that arise for some people that can have an impact on the positive experience of practicing Acro. Each person's concerns may be related to physical aspects of the practice, emotional traumas that get triggered, or societal impacts of the community. Raising awareness of these concerns can help you and members of the community have a more compassionate understanding of the people you may be training and playing with. Some frequently mentioned concerns are discussed in this section, but this is by no means a comprehensive list. You should always remain open to acknowledging additional concerns that are brought up by the people in your life.

The leaders of Acro communities hold the value of inclusiveness highly. Consequently, there are always initiatives to make sure that people have groups to work with in jams and classes, along with offering material that can be approachable for people of any body type. Nevertheless, although most Acro spaces are not exclusionary, there may still be inherent and societal barriers to accessibility. It takes a significant amount of free time to continue improving in the practice. Being able to get to the spaces where other people are training and playing can sometimes be a troubling obstacle. If training times clash with a work schedule, or the training space requires an hour-long commute, it can be difficult to attend on a weekly basis. In addition, going to jams and events that are not located at parks, may require additional financial costs; each person needs to decide what fits within their financial ability or budget. Keeping up with the pace of advancement within an Acro community can create pressure that pushes members to either commit or, possibly, fall off.

Because Acro involves lifting people, there can be preferential treatment of certain people based on body size and appearance. For the people who desire to be lifted into the air, the Flyers, those with smaller bodies or who appear to be thinner or lighter, may be approached to partner up more often than others and may be encouraged to try more difficult skills. It's important to recognize and validate the biases that certain people may experience, so that we don't knowingly exacerbate any trauma felt by any person. For Bases, the people who desire to lift others into the air, people who appear to be stronger, or to have more masculine bodies, may get approached to partner up more often than others and also often have their perspective listened to over other people involved in the group. When this comes up for a person, it is beneficial to have someone either within the community or outside, to whom they can turn in order to share their frustrations or be reassured.

> *"My main insecurity these days is about my limitations as an acrobat. I'm proud of the progress I've made in both ground and standing Acro, but my body has limitations*

because of past injuries and not enough free time to weight train for bigger skills. Sometimes I worry people don't want to partner with me because I can't keep pushing into new levels. But that feels absurd, because the reason I joined Acro in the first place was community. That brings up an important point: everyone does Acro for different reasons. If folks want to push edges and level up, that's totally fine and should be encouraged. But for those seeking community and supportive relationships, the tricks and edges aren't as critical. Identifying goals with others, whether in jams, classes, or private practice, is so damn important. There's a lot less confusion and miscommunication when everyone is on the same page." –C.S., Seattle Acro Community

When any of these types of triggering events happen, it is important to have people you can trust and rely on to support you when working through the emotional burdens. Later in this book, we will go over how to identify them in your current relationships and develop this trust and support in your attachment-based relationships. You can also develop support systems within yourself, which will be covered later in the book.

In the ways that interactions in Acro are a microcosm of the kinds of relationship dynamics experienced in other areas of our lives, each of us can find a great sense of wonder to benefit us every day. A large reason why we have focused on expanding secure relationships within Acro partnerships is the values that are embraced within the Acro community. Some of the values that we have found significant in the Acro community overlap with the studies and framework for secure-relationship building. While not all the relationships in our lives are built around playfulness, there are elements of enjoyment and reward in all of our valued relationships. Bringing the element of play into the significant relationships in our lives can improve the enjoyment and desire we have in the relationships that matter to us. By embracing and practicing the values we find in Acro communities, we can bring that trust and those learnings into all the relationships in our lives.

Notes

1. *B. Thomas, "A Brief History of Acroyoga: The Origin & Roots of Acrobatic Yoga," Slackrobats, July 19, 2017.*
2. *Simon Sinek, "Asking for Help Is an Act of Service," video, Brilliant Minds Foundation, June 2024.*

2

Playing Within Acro Relationships

Embracing playfulness within a regular practice invites more spontaneity and often opens the door to interacting with a wider range of people. Exploring movement with different partners can help you notice which interactions feel enjoyable, energizing, or especially compelling. Over time, you may find yourself drawn to certain people more consistently, whether because of the quality of your communication, the way your bodies work together, or simply how you feel in their presence. Play also gives you space to try different ways of relating and to notice how those choices are received. As you reflect on your own experience, you may begin to recognize that some partnerships leave you wanting more time together, while others feel better in smaller doses. When you are flying or basing with particular people, do you find yourself wanting to continue playing with them, or do you notice a limit to how much time you want to spend together in a session? Paying attention to those responses can help you better understand what kinds of interactions feel most supportive, engaging, and meaningful to you.

The act of play strengthens communication, resilience, and trustworthiness. It encourages examining the present moment rather than comparing it to past experiences or future expectations. There are different kinds of play that we can engage in. According to Rene Proyer's research,[1] four types of playfulness are other-directed playfulness, which involves good-natured teasing of other people; lighthearted playfulness, which involves seeing life as more like a game than a battlefield; intellectual playfulness, where we play with ideas and solve puzzles; and whimsical playfulness, which involves unusual activities and imitating people or objects. All of these types of playfulness can be experienced through Acro movement and interactions. Play fosters creativity, and in turn, creativity stimulates playfulness.

Through play, we are able to learn the art of letting go by detaching from the sense that actions are directed personally. Stepping into a playful mindset typically creates emotional space between the situation and how it ties to our personal identity. In this space, there is room for choice in how our persona should respond and whether the moment is significant to a larger purpose. If the playful situation does not need to be significantly purposeful, we tend to be able to let it go as simply "a moment." This capacity for letting go assists us in and out of our relationships. Being right becomes less important when we've centered play. We can admit when we messed up if the moment is not tied to our sense of identity. In centering around play, the knowledge that there's an us, separate from either of us, is worth tending to.

Playfulness in Acro Lends to Establishing Attachment Quickly

Often in Acro environments, you jump into playing or practicing with someone with very little introduction or small talk. There's something profoundly transformative about striving together toward a shared goal, pushing through obstacles, riding the surge of adrenaline in the face of challenge, celebrating the sweet triumph of success, or finding joy in the laughter that follows failure. Whether you are able to master the skill or collapse in a heap of laughter at a spectacular misstep, it's in these raw, unfiltered, and often playful moments that powerful bonds are forged. The shared experience of overcoming challenges creates a powerful emotional connection. You may leave this experience feeling very bonded and connected with this person you just met.

Acro relationships can often feel accelerated to an intimate or vulnerable level very quickly because of the nature of Acro. You are being asked to trust another person. You are engaged in continual physical touch and trying new activities, often outside of your comfort zone. This practice brings out individuals' strengths and weaknesses very quickly. Areas of communication, consent, body awareness, focus, and trustworthiness are immediately exposed, often with very little knowledge of who this person is. Even without this knowledge, there are many elements that support your feelings of comfort and safety. Being vulnerable with the body can influence being vulnerable with emotions. You can have a short interaction with someone in Acro and, in that short time, feel very close and connected with them.

The chemical processes in the body can respond powerfully to the kinds of play, touch, and challenge that happen in Acro. Sustained physical contact with another person can stimulate the release of **oxytocin**, a neurotransmitter associated with bonding, trust, and feelings of closeness. In the early stages of connection, this can help people feel more comfortable, more attuned, and more open around certain partners. At the same time, working through a challenge, especially one that feels difficult or intimidating, can bring a strong sense of accomplishment when you succeed or make progress. That experience is often linked with **dopamine**, a neurotransmitter associated with reward, motivation, and satisfaction. Together, these responses can make Acro interactions feel emotionally significant very quickly, sometimes creating feelings of attachment or closeness sooner than people find in other kinds of relationships.[2]

While these neurochemicals and experiences can feel like there is an attachment to another person, the foundations of an attachment-based relationship may not yet have been put in place. There needs to be room to enjoy this feeling, without basing decisions on that feeling alone. As you become aware of the emotional influences that your time in Acro has on your personal experience, it can also be important to delve deeper into how the other areas of your life are emotionally influencing your daily experience and feelings of attachment.

Relationship Structure vs Emotional Experience

One of the areas that is often confronted when people deepen their Acro practice and their ties with the community, is how they approach their relationships in the community, along with their relationships in the rest of their lives. As some people are exposed to different kinds of relationships within their Acro experience, their beliefs about relationship dynamics may be challenged. Depending on personal relationship histories, Acro norms can bring up conflicting thoughts that touch on beliefs regarding the actions that may be sacredly reserved for specific kinds of relationships, such as with romantic partners. The ways you may interact with someone whom you are trusting with your physical well-being may mimic some of the ways that you interact with significant romantic or familial partners. What does it mean for you when some actions or habits, typically reserved for romantic or life partners, are being shared in other relationships? Does that diminish the significance of those relationships at all, or can it enrich your understanding of why you continue to choose those significant relationships in your life?

The quality of your personally significant relationships is important to examine from a different perspective when the circumstances of your life are in a period of change. In addition to the beliefs you have about your intimate relationships, take time to examine how you feel about it. First examine your experience based only on the ways the other person treats you and then on how you feel about them during your interactions. These may be difficult to separate depending on your beliefs about relationships and what you are expected to gain from them. For many people, the structure of a relationship provides much of their security and positive self-impressions rather than their internal relational experience. When you strip away all external influences and focus solely on what each of you contributes, *how strong is the quality of your relationship?* For the significant relationships in your life, *if there were no financial expectations, no pressure to be together, and no advantages tied to either person's status or role, would the connection still feel just as fulfilling and aligned with your lifestyle?* As you examine the quality of your relational experience, there are many factors you can reflect on. Here are several different assumptions that come up around relationships that can be reexamined so you can establish your own beliefs, separate from those imposed by your society.

The idea in traditional cultures that only intimate partners touch the areas of the body between the shoulders and knees is confronted mightily when witnessing the platonic touch shared during many acrobatic poses. Touch is both a desirable and needed element of the human experience. In accordance with modern societal expectations, many people aim to satisfy their needs for touch only within their romantic relationships. This can put significant pressure on our romantic relationships, especially if either partner is not ready or able to provide this element. There can be so much variability in how much touch is comfortable for each person in a relationship, as well as the timing of when each person is receptive to touch. For your own relationships, *are you able to give or receive enough physical touch to satisfy your needs and desires? What would your relationships look like if you were able to satisfy your need for touch from more than just relationships that were romantic or sexual in nature? Would that change your approach to connection within those relationships?*

The idea that romantic partners should spend most of their free time together is a fairly recent societal expectation in North American culture. When your romantic partner is treated as the person you are supposed to spend most of your time with, the relationship can begin to shape or limit how you imagine your time should be spent. Are you spending most of your time together because it feels expected, without considering other possibilities, or because being together brings genuine enjoyment and satisfaction? It is also worth considering whether or not the time you spend together is meeting each other's needs and whether the quality of that time could be improved. Reflecting on these questions can help clarify whether the relationship feels more valuable because of the genuine meaning, nourishment, and connection it brings to your life, rather than simply because of an inherited expectation about how partners are supposed to spend their time.

Becoming financially intertwined together is seen as a significant signal of a committed relationship in more traditional cultures. How do your relationships stack up when finances are considered separate and the evaluation is based on other factors? Conversely, *who are the people you base your decision-making on? Who are you asking for direct input, feedback, and consideration as you make lifestyle decisions?* The amount of priority you give these people shows which relationships matter most in your life. For many traditional relationship structures, committed romantic partners and family served as core pillars for lifestyle choices. With more recent changes in North American societal structures, the emergence of professional and non-familial relationships have become more significant considerations for lifestyle choices. Within your life, how will you consider the relationships you have as you make decisions about your own priorities?

There are many qualities that can make a relationship feel meaningful enough to deserve deep commitment. In many social narratives surrounding committed romantic relationships, having and raising children is seen as both a major responsibility and a central source of purpose. For many couples of previous generations, the meaning of long-term commitment was closely connected to the task of raising children together. This may have carried particular weight within a Western capitalist context, where child-rearing often became centered within the household, rather than shared across a broader village, neighborhood, or community. If the responsibility for raising children were more widely shared in a community, how might the role and significance of romantic partnership shift in your life, and how might you choose to express that significance?

Do you need titles for your relationship to feel significant? Would you feel like the relationship matters more to the other person more if they called you their "girlfriend/boyfriend" versus the "person they are dating"? *Does the element of having a title or label for your relationship provide a sense of certainty or security?* What meaning do those labels hold for you and what beliefs are tied to those relationship statuses? Are there certain actions that you expect from the other person in the relationship simply because they give you a title, and not because you explicitly discussed any responsibilities? Unless the two of you grew up from childhood in the same community with similar societal conditioning, or shared the same relationship examples, the titles you agree to may have very different meanings and expectations. While relationships with labels can imply levels of commitment, it is the conversations, negotiations, and agreements you have in your relationships that establish the commitments that you both can depend on.

You shouldn't rely solely on the structure of relationships for security. Knowing that you are prioritized on one or more of these dimensions should not replace the quality of your interpersonal experience. If certain emotional needs are not being satisfied by one relationship, you should not limit yourself to trying to get all of those needs met by that same relationship. This doesn't necessarily need to be a reason to end a relationship in order to try and find a better one. You can lean on and enrich other relationships in your life to help satisfy your emotional needs. As we dive deeper into attachment-based relationships and strengthening those bonds, we will see how relationship structure and relationship quality are separate elements. While the structure of a relationship can create a container for interactions to occur more often and with less direction, the experience of those interactions is much more impactful on the quality and satisfaction of our relationships. We will cover in more depth how to keep these kinds of relationships secure in later chapters. For now, we want to normalize that the tension that occurs in your established relationships while you are deepening your connections in Acro is not unjustified and can be addressed with mutual care and respect.

Emotional Attunement - Are Your Relationships FED?

As you are becoming more aware of your interactions and your place in your relationships, it can be helpful to understand whether you want to nourish those relationships or create space from negative interactions. Being able to make a conscious and informed decision about your intention in relationships can improve the quality and enjoyment of your relationships. Answering this question will help bring more awareness: *Are your relationships FED?:* Have you set intentions for your relationships to be fortified, escalating, or depreciated?

Relationship Fortification: As you experience each of the relationships in your life, there may be many that you enjoy or feel content in by the ways that they show up in your life. This could be a friend you see monthly at a sports league or club. It could also be the acquaintance you see working at the grocery store whenever you visit. You may not want these relationships to change significantly. These would be the relationships that you should fortify and embrace in the ways they currently are. These relationships may not need to be significantly invested in, but having an awareness of gratitude for these relationships will help keep them from unintentionally degrading or falling apart. Let these people know that you appreciate them for the ways that they show up in your life and ensure that they also feel positively about how you both currently show up for each other. This intention of reassurance can have a significant impact on fortifying these relationships.

Relationship Escalation: In some of your relationships, you might notice yourself naturally choosing to spend time with certain people over others. There may be a pull to stay longer in their presence, or an instinctive urge to be around particular people. When you are not in that person's presence, do you feel an emotional or cognitive pull to reach out to them? In relationships with these individuals, you might feel a desire for things to deepen; to grow closer, spend more time together, and take the connection to the next level, whether right away or gradually over time. As you spend time with them, *do you feel valued and seen? Are they investing their time and energy into you and your wants?* As relationship coach Matthew Hussey says,[3] "Invest in those who invest in you." *Are they matching the effort you're putting into your interactions, or even reaching out on their own to check in with you?* If they're showing genuine interest in your thoughts and feelings, it could be a sign that the relationship has the potential to grow into something more. These are relationships that you want to escalate and nourish. Having a conversation to discover each of your intentions and comfort with the relationship can create more fulfillment in it. We will cover how to establish a more intentional relationship in later chapters.

Relationship Depreciation: In other cases, you may feel like you have spent as much time with another person as you can tolerate. You may even want to create space from them. This doesn't necessarily have to result from a negative experience. Nor do the feelings need to be negatively extreme. Not all relationships have to be embraced, and it can be healthy and normal to move a relationship toward depreciation. You can consciously decline more interactions with a person and oppose investing additional time into those relationships. No matter how long you have been part of a relationship, there is no principle that prevents a relationship from being depreciated, only the beliefs of the people involved. For established relationships, or those with a sense of commitment, communicating that the relationship will be depreciated can be healthy etiquette and provide clear boundaries for the relationship moving forward. If you feel the need to avoid someone, feel unsafe around them, or have already stopped speaking to them for a prolonged time, it's perfectly reasonable not to explain why the relationship is fading. In any case, setting your own intention of depreciating the relationship can free you up for the other relationships in your life.

Are You Beginning to Get Emotionally Close?

As you spend more time with someone and the connection begins to deepen, it's helpful to check in with yourself and consider the emotional dynamics at play. One way to do this is by noticing the emotional comfort of your interactions. *Is there a sense of genuine acceptance or curiosity between you? Do you feel comfortable sharing parts of yourself, such as your thoughts, stories, and even your vulnerabilities, without fearing judgment?* A key sign of emotional safety is the ability to listen and respond without becoming triggered or reactive. When both people can remain open and present, even during emotionally charged conversations, it suggests a healthy foundation. But if your emotional comfort becomes heavily tied to their reactions or approval, it could indicate a growing emotional dependence.

Trust also plays a big role in how emotionally tethered we become. In Acro or similar practices, physical trust is a common gateway to emotional closeness. Notice your own thoughts or sensations when practicing: *Do you feel secure letting this person spot you or guide you through movement?* Beyond just preventing falls, trust can extend to subtler things, like feeling confident that they're attuned to the environment and your needs within it. For instance, *if you were to close your eyes and let them lead you around a room, would you feel safe?* These moments of surrender can create strong emotional bonds, but they can also blur the line between healthy connection and emotional dependency if your sense of safety starts relying solely on their presence.

It's equally important to notice how you feel when you're not around them. If you find yourself feeling anxious, insecure, or unsettled when they're with other people or focused elsewhere, it may point to a developing attachment that is rooted more in emotional need than mutual connection. Feeling disappointed or missing someone is natural, but if their absence consistently triggers worry or possessiveness, that is a signal to explore your emotional boundaries. Do you feel incomplete without them, or can you hold onto your sense of self even when they're not immediately available?

Becoming emotionally close to someone is not inherently

unhealthy; it's a natural and often beautiful part of deepening relationships. However, emotional dependency can arise when your well-being becomes overly reliant on how the other person behaves or responds. Regular self-reflection and open communication can help you stay aware of how your connection is evolving, and whether it is fostering mutual growth or leaning too heavily in one direction. Emotional security within a relationship starts with emotional awareness within yourself.

With the relationship awareness you have built for yourself through these principles, you can begin to take action to preserve or develop the relationships you choose for your life. While these principles can be practiced and implemented more quickly in Acro environments, the same choices can be examined and made within relationships in other areas of your life. Becoming more consciously decisive about the relationships you develop in the professional and social areas of your life can alleviate excessive stress. This gives you space to put your time and energy into the people who will help you enjoy or progress in those areas of your life. One of the big takeaways that we would like to impart from this book and your time in the Acro community is this: Do not take the relationships in your life for granted. When you discover positive, satisfying interactions and experiences that feel good, use that new awareness to benefit the existing areas of your life. Your relationships have the ability to change and you can keep updating each of your relationships as you change throughout your life.

Notes

1. *René T. Proyer, "A New Structural Model for the Study of Adult Playfulness: Assessment and Exploration of an Understudied Individual Differences Variable," Personality and Individual Differences 108 (2017): 113–22.*

2. *Andreas Bartels and Semir Zeki, "The Neural Basis of Romantic Love," NeuroReport 11, no. 17 (2000): 3829–34.*

3. *Matthew Hussey, "How to Know If You Should Keep Trying with Him," MatthewHussey.com, November 7, 2020.*

3

Developing Your Own Acro Relationships

Getting to experience the wonder of play within Acro and enjoying all the people you meet through the practice opens up so many possibilities. At times, when some connections feel easy, it's full of light-hearted conversations and shared laughter over inside jokes that pop up out of nowhere. This eases the tension of trying something new. When parting ways, there may be a lingering sense of warmth. There can also be a quiet ache, a wish for more: more time, more depth, or a wish to trade quick catch-ups for deeper interactions. It is not necessarily romantic, just the yearning for a deeper partnership, something grounded and reliable. When you wonder how to ask for more without making it feel like too much, it's time for courage. It's time to build a bridge to navigate the space in between. As you experience more moments of flow and success in your practice and discover training partners you genuinely enjoy, turning that fun into a consistent, reliable relationship can ease some of the uncertainty.

Within the Acro space, there may be dynamics that can stimulate feelings of attachment and attraction. Identify when those feelings may be based on the situation rather than the dynamics with another person. Once you have become more aware of the relationships that you want to escalate, find out where you and the other person stand in the relationship. Are there any existing power dynamics or obligations? Are you already depending on that person or becoming preemptively attached to them before they have consented?

When you are able to discover the relational awareness discussed in the previous chapter, you will be able to take action more consciously. You can take steps to transition those chosen relationships to be more conscious Acro relationships. In the following sections, we will dive more into the behaviors that are helpful for the Acro relationships you want in your life.

Building Rapport and a Sense of Connection

Having an enjoyable connection with another person does not always happen by serendipity. There are many factors that come into play. Either person can consciously encourage a sense of rapport that leads to connection. While practicing Acro, we are each adapting to and calibrating with the other person's physicality, whether consciously or subconsciously. Working to complement each other's sense of power, speed, and enthusiasm is a key part of finding successes within different movements in Acro. In the earlier stages, mirroring each other's physicality can create a sense of mutual involvement. Matching each other's engagement helps both people feel invested in the interaction and that they're both working toward a shared outcome. As you become more advanced in this calibration, learning to complement each other's physicality can lead to more dynamic interactions without losing rapport. This may mean momentarily pushing less while the other person pushes more. It may also mean staying stable at the connection point where they can add power, or adding your own power into another connection point where they have stability. This requires awareness. So as not to overpower the other person, you need to have an idea of where they may have more ability to engage, while avoiding the points where they are more vulnerable. The sense of connection and success that is felt when there is a strong level of rapport is magnified. These same strategies can also be applied to interactions outside of Acro, in areas such as voice tone, pace, physical posture, and eye contact.

Mirroring someone's tone, pace, and physicality is a subtle yet powerful way to communicate empathy and create an atmosphere of emotional safety. When you naturally reflect how someone is behaving, you send a nonverbal message that says, *"I'm in sync with you."* This isn't about mimicry, but rather about creating a subtle rapport that puts both people at ease. Our bodies respond in reaction to this feeling of comfort and connection. People are naturally more comfortable around others who reflect back their physical and emotional energy. It signals that you're paying attention, that you're not just talking with them, but also feeling with them. Ultimately, rapport is about creating a space where the other person feels seen, safe, and respected. Afterward, each of you may walk away from the interaction with a sense of being respected and valued. It's in these often unnoticed, intentional behaviors that the foundation for genuine connection is nonverbally built.

By engaging in these moments where understanding is being developed between people, a shared reality is created. This shared reality can be developed as we get to know each other and the environment better. There may be a shared reality among all the people within a community, and also a subsequent shared reality between smaller groups of people in the community. Creating a shared reality in our relationships involves building a mutual understanding of the world we all experience—emotionally, mentally, and physically. Two actions you can take to contribute to this shared reality are 1) openly discussing your thoughts, feelings, values, and goals, and 2) being curious about your partner's experience. They both help establish a shared understanding. Instead of assuming shared alignment, take time to ask questions like, *"How did that feel for you?"* or *"What does that mean to you?"* This ongoing curiosity helps each person feel seen and reduces the chances of misunderstanding.

Participation in a shared reality in a community can lend itself to a shared reality within a partnership. Another powerful tactic for contributing to a community's shared reality is co-creating routines, vocabulary, and rituals that are common among everyone in the community. Sharing experiences, whether it's tackling a challenge together, celebrating a small win, or even establishing inside jokes, also plays a key role in creating a common sense of connection and rapport. Having a shared understanding fosters a sense of continuity, predictability, and belonging, reinforcing the idea that you're working together toward a common outcome, not just existing side-by-side. With a shared reality, everyone involved contributes toward the cultural landscape, and in doing so, deepens their connection, understanding, and sense of partnership.

Evaluating the Potential for Deeper Connection

When you notice shared commonalities and enjoyment with another person, the feelings for connection may peak. Examining the dynamic of a connection before transitioning it into an intentional relationship is helpful, because it reveals whether or not the potential is open enough to support deeper emotional investment. A healthy connection involves more than shared interests; it includes mutual respect, ease of communication, emotional safety, and appropriate responsiveness. When you take the time to observe how naturally you relate, how well you handle challenges together, and how emotionally fulfilling your interactions are, you gain clarity on whether the relationship can grow in a healthy, sustainable way. Without this groundwork, moving into a more intentional dynamic may feel forced or lead to unmet expectations. Exploring these topics ahead of time helps reduce disappointment and ensures that deepening the relationship is a natural evolution, not a leap built on hope alone.

As you consider whether or not this connection is one you'd like to deepen, it's important to evaluate how you both handle conflict or moments of tension. Pay attention to how you respond to each other when progress stalls. When a new skill isn't clicking, or one of you is having an off day, how does that affect your shared goals? Do you approach these situations collaboratively, focusing on finding a solution together, or do you get stuck dwelling on what went wrong? Notice whether or not emotional safety is maintained during these moments. Do you still feel comfortable being yourself and expressing how you feel? Can you be vulnerable without fear of judgment or withdrawal? And just as importantly, is there room for levity? Being able to laugh together, even in frustration, can be a powerful indicator of resilience and emotional alignment. These experiences offer valuable insight into the foundation of your connection and whether it has the strength to support something more.

When you have both the capacity and the desire to rely on someone, your sensitivity to their presence and needs often increases, and the same can happen in return. You may find yourself more attuned to their bids for connection, such as picking up on the sound of their voice even in a noisy room, or noticing when they're glancing around for something they've misplaced. These small moments of awareness are signs of deeper attunement and care. You might also find yourself instinctively leaning into their touch when they reach out to get your attention, responding more naturally and effortlessly to their nonverbal cues. This kind of responsiveness often emerges when you're emotionally open and "primed" for connection, exhibiting when your nervous system feels safe and receptive in their presence. It becomes easier to notice the subtle ways they reach out, and to respond with warmth, presence, and engagement. These micro-moments of connection, though small, are powerful building blocks in deepening trust and rapport, helping to create a dynamic where both people feel seen, valued, and connected.

Sometimes you may need to ask yourself, *Should this relationship expand outside of this particular Acro space?* Just because you enjoy working with someone doesn't mean that you are in alignment to be consistent Acro partners, and that is okay. A very healthy perspective in a casual Acro environment is to enjoy the connections that you make, even if they only happen one time. Every individual creates an opportunity for you to learn something about yourself and grow your Acro practice. Once you have gained some awareness of the degree to which each of you are open to deepening your Acro practice with a more intentional relationship, you may need more tools to find and explore the idea with other people.

Exploring the Idea of a New Partnership

When you and a partner have been interacting in Acro spaces and experiencing the heightened thrills with each other, this may give only a partial perspective of an enjoyable connection. Sometimes you may not have been able to interact with each other outside of this space very often. As you prepare to escalate a relationship, you may need to examine whether or not it should expand outside of the Acro space. Will you need to create a new shared reality together? How do each of you interpret the realities that you already live in? Can you communicate how you can navigate these realities together?

Bringing the other person into the conversation should be done separately from Acro activities, although it may be more palatable to offer the invitation to the conversation during your time playing with each other. It may be preferable to step away from the Acro space during a jam or training so you can go right back to the Acro activity afterwards.

As you invite the other person to have a conversation, give enough time and multiple opportunities to explore all elements of the idea to expand the relationship. The conversation to explore this should be done over multiple interactions. It doesn't need to be done all in one conversation. Early on, you may want to take time to find out each other's level of enthusiasm and comfort with commitments. Sharing enthusiasm with positive reinforcement is always a good place to start. If you enjoy practicing with someone, tell them why, and be specific. Have a clear up-front conversation with the person.

As you delve into these conversations, find out each other's desires for their Acro practice and what each of you values highly in the activity. There may be a lot of enthusiasm for learning new skills, or getting to connect with the community, or teaching skills or classes to others. Your excitements within Acro don't need to be the same, but there should be some alignment that will incentivize each of you to lean further into the relationship. If one of you wants to learn new Acro skills and the other wants to find security and safety while playing, having a trusted and calibrated partner would elevate both of your practices. Conversely, if one of you mainly wants to be social within the community, while the other wants to master Acro skills, the time needed for repeated repetitions may take away from the chances to have social interactions and meet new people. This conflict in interests could cause friction as each of you tries to fulfill your desires.

There may also be many practicalities and logistics that you will need to figure out with each other. In order to increase the time you want to spend together, you will have to figure out when your schedules line up and what routines are already part of each other's weeks. It may be as simple as finding out whether both of you will be at the same Acro classes or jams, or it may involve finding new times and locations to meet up. Do each of you live geographically close enough to meet up routinely? Will there be time available outside of work and other obligations?

After you have established that there is interest in practicing together and available opportunities to meet, go a step deeper to understand what the major priorities in each of your lives are and where this developing relationship would sit with among those priorities. Will each of you still have time to meet if work gets busier or friends invite you to another activity? Would either of you choose to spend your time elsewhere if given equal opportunities? This does not necessarily diminish the value of the relationship, but it gives better expectations for how you'll handle changes in your lives. As long as you both understand how you will approach your time practicing with each other, it can improve future communication and reduce unspoken disappointments. These types of specific questions are going to give you deeper insight into the intentions of this individual and help you know whether the two of you would make a good Acro partnership. Depending on each of your levels of commitment and priorities, there are several types of relationships that you can build into.

Different Approaches to Relationships in Acro

Within the Acro community, people regularly encounter and interact with a broad circle of others. Not all the people that a person sees regularly have to become a significant relationship. There are many different types of beneficial relationships that can form with other people in a class, jam, or community, each of which can be valued.

Here are five of the most common types of Acro relationships. You do not need to establish which kind of relationship you would like in one conversation, and discussing each kind of relationship does not need to be in isolation. Each of these kinds of relationships are not mutually exclusive from each other. Many of them can overlap in multiple aspects. Also, the different kinds of Acro relationships are not limited to those listed here, and not all relationships have to be escalated into another kind of relationship.

Friends of Convenience

At a simple level, some relationships are **friendships of convenience**: people you see often in certain environments and enjoy being around while you are there. These are relationships that thrive when two people run into each other organically and often their conversations continue or revolve around a specific activity or topic. Much of the time, there isn't a significant effort to schedule time to see each other outside of the environment where both people met. And there isn't a feeling of loss by not spending time together otherwise. These relationships can be beneficial for each person in creating a sense of comfort and familiarity while enjoying specific activities or events. Seeing familiar people with some regularity can create a sense of safety and steadiness, making it easier to enter environments that might otherwise feel uncertain or unfamiliar.

Cohort Peers

Since Acro is a practice with significant cumulative growth and skill development, there are often many people of different skill levels practicing in one shared space. A lot of proactive communication is used to figure out and assess each person's experience and their comfort level with each skill. Because of the continual effort to assess each situation, it can be enjoyable to practice with people who share a similar skill level and experience. People who started their Acro practice around the same time or in the same classes are called **cohort peers**. It can feel comforting to stick together and form a bond that will be reinforced as they take more classes together. Even though a person may see these people repeatedly, it doesn't mean that they inherently become friends or know about each other's lives or interests. Through this kind of relationship, there is a significant feeling of familiarity and, potentially, a sense of rivalry that pushes each other to continue improving.

Training Partners

Training together on a regular basis, whether in classes or smaller group settings, can turn shared practice into a meaningful bond. These people can become **training partners**. There are many aspects that become important when both people actively consent to becoming training partners. While developing a good sense of safety between both people is important, this does not have to be a relationship that expands outside of training. These kinds of relationships typically encourage the growth of each person in the partnership and may include shared objectives for the relationship.

> *"My experience was primarily with performing groups, usually 4 to 13 acrobats, with 6 being the average. Performing-group dynamics are a whole crazy subject of their own. I never really went the route of sustaining a single reliable Acro partner, since I trained dozens of Flyers and Mids every year and could kinda take my pick for partner work. But there is something to be said for consistent, mostly exclusive stunt partners." — S.P., Pacific Northwest Community*

Teaching or Performance Partners

These are extensions of the training relationship. If there is a particular objective to the training partnership, such as teaching classes or preparing for performing together, then the relationship can have a shared purpose. That shared purpose can elevate the partnership, giving it greater weight, clearer expectations, and a deeper level of interdependence than a more casual training relationship. It takes time to build a shared vocabulary and the trust to perform skills consistently under any circumstance. A whole culture of movement style and training habits need to be developed, especially when the goal is to make it clear to an outside audience what they are trying to convey. When **teaching or performance partners** begin traveling together, the added pressure and proximity can magnify tensions and make relational misalignments harder to ignore. When teaching or performing together, they will have to be able to maintain a calm and steady state in order to reach the results of their training.

Romantic and Play Partners

Expanding a relationship to include romantic intentions can feel both natural and nuanced, especially when it begins in a space of shared activity, like Acro or movement training. While the emotional connection may already be strong, layering in romantic interest introduces new dynamics that can ripple into other parts of the relationship. It's important to approach this shift thoughtfully, as the emotional stakes often grow and can impact not only your personal connection but also the broader community (if you both share the same social or training circles).

Romantic relationships that also include **play partnerships** occupy a unique space in Acro communities. They are a blending of personal desires with social and cultural expectations. Choosing to go on one-on-one outings, share more exclusive time together, or engage in physical affection beyond platonic touch can signal a move into romantic territory. If sexual intimacy becomes part of the relationship, clear and ongoing consent is essential, along with conversations about comfort, boundaries, and desires. This type of relationship doesn't necessarily require long-term commitment, but it does require honest dialogue and clarity about emotional safety and intentions. In a close-knit community, where relational dynamics often overlap, addressing these needs openly can help prevent misunderstandings, protect emotional well-being, and support a more respectful and caring environment for everyone involved.

Dealing with Fears and Feelings of Rejection

The prospect of asking for a change in the relationship dynamic can cause anxiety to surface that is shaped not only by the relationship itself, but also by broader emotional patterns and past experiences. Fears can creep in or be triggered when you start thinking about the other person's reactions and whether they will reject your attempt at connection. These fears of rejection can also come up when we are at an Acro jam and want to ask another person to play, or try a skill for the first (or hundredth) time. If the other person says no, or plans don't work out, individuals can feel rejected. The fear of this rejection can be felt more severely than the actual rejection. It can show up as bodily feelings or emotional sensations.

This may present as body rejection, and the rejection can trigger past thoughts or stories of being the wrong size or weight for the role they wish to play. It can also manifest as emotional rejection, as it can feel vulnerable to ask to work with someone or partner up. An individual may feel that the other person doesn't like their personality, or who they are, and this can feel very hurtful. It can take time to deal with these fears of rejection and to address the triggers of the fears, but while being in the middle of these interactions there are various ways that you can move through the feelings. Keeping your mind focused on your desired outcome or the reason you are reaching out, focusing on your breath, or acting before the fears become overwhelming are all methods of distraction away from the fear. Building up positive feelings is another strategy for addressing these fears.

Establishing a sense of confidence around what you have to offer, such as your Acro knowledge, experience, or ability to create a fun and engaging interaction, can help outweigh the fear of rejection. One way to build this confidence in Acro-jam settings is figuring out an Acro skill or washing machine that you know well, enjoy, and are willing to share with others. You can offer to share skills as a way to start a play session or interaction. As you become comfortable engaging others with this offering, you will strengthen a skill that builds positive connections. You may even become sought after to share that skill with others in a jam or training space. When you reach out to another person to try something new that you may not be as confident about, you will have something to fall back on if your invitation is turned down.

Reducing the fear of ostracization can minimize aspects of the fear of rejection. By becoming more acquainted with the culture of your community and having one or more strong bonds with other members of the community, you can gain such a sense of security that an instance of rejection won't cause the loss of your inclusion in the community. Establishing a friendly connection with one of the teachers within your community can also provide a more stable bond with the community, such that you know there will be a space for you within the community.

When rejection happens, it's important to remember that it's rarely a personal judgment of you. There are countless reasons behind someone's decision that you may never fully understand. Most of those reasons have everything to do with their own experiences, boundaries, or current state of mind, and very little to do with you, or what you offered. The rejection is personal to them, not you. Keeping this perspective can help you stay grounded and resilient in your Acro journey. Everyone enters this practice with their own set of traumas, insecurities, preferences, and limitations. When someone says no, cancels plans, or falls short of your expectations, it's not a reflection of your worth or effort. It simply means they are honoring their own needs, and you can do the same by not internalizing it. Letting go of the need to take things personally allows you to stay open, flexible, and focused on what truly matters: growth, connection, and joy in the practice.

These are only a few of the methods that can be utilized to deal with the fears and feelings of rejection. Leaning into the positive aspects of yourself and your community are the most powerful strategies for moving through the fears of rejection and enhancing your relationship with yourself. Additional methods for navigating these moments will be covered later in the book as we share strategies for trigger management in Chapter 11.

Establishing an Acro partnership often requires more thought and effort than we initially realize, especially when the goal is to build something healthy and intentional. It's not just about finding someone who can base or fly well; it's also about identifying potential partners with whom you feel mutual trust, communication, and alignment. Taking the time to genuinely explore those connections and reflect on what makes them strong can significantly increase your chances of creating fulfilling relationships. Being clear and intentional in how you invite someone into the idea of a partnership can also prevent misunderstandings, manage expectations, and reduce future disappointments. Strong Acro partnerships have the potential to become a deeply rewarding part of your life, adding not just skill and progress, but joy, support, and personal growth.

When we each cultivate healthy, respectful relationships within our Acro communities, the ripple effect naturally shapes the broader community and its culture. Many of the values that define the Acro community today, such as consent, proactive communication, inclusivity, and emotional awareness, were not always emphasized when the practice first took form in 2003. These values have grown out of the lived experiences of partnerships within the community, evolving as practitioners shared, adapted, and refined what felt supportive and empowering. In this way, every intentional connection contributes to a more positive, supportive community. And when it feels good to be part of that community, we not only thrive in our own practice, but we are also more likely to invite others in with confidence, joy, and care.

Part II

As we've progressed in our Acro journeys, one of the things that has become increasingly clear is how deeply our growth is tied to the strength of our relationships within the community. We've seen that when Spotters in a community develop more advanced awareness and reliability, the skill level of everyone tends to rise. Similarly, the overall health and longevity of a community often reflect the values and resilience found in its core relationships. When people begin to open themselves to the joy, connection, and vulnerability that Acro invites, it's almost inevitable that deeper, more meaningful relationships begin to form. These relationships can often look and feel different from those we may have experienced in other areas of our lives.

In building partnerships, whether for a single flow, or a

long-term Acro connection, we begin to engage more intentionally with others. But what does it really mean to establish a relationship within this space? What are we bringing into these connections from our past experiences? And how might we carry that forward into all of our relationships with greater awareness?

Many of us have felt the impact of our relationships in both evident and subtle ways. Sometimes, we clearly see how someone's support has helped us grow. Other times, we may simply feel more grounded, inspired, or challenged when they're around. Our past relationships, both inside and outside Acro, shape how we approach new ones, as to what we expect, how we communicate, and what we believe we deserve. When we've felt unfulfilled in certain areas, we may have sought connection elsewhere, hoping to feel seen, supported, or simply understood. These patterns often emerge in our Acro partnerships too, whether we're aware of them or not.

If someone hasn't experienced a strong sense of belonging in their early relationships, such as with family, they might seek that sense of belonging in friendships or communities. Ideally, this leads to building healthier habits and more nourishing relationships. But when our needs continue to go unmet, it's also common to respond by overextending ourselves, minimizing our desires, or settling for less than what we truly hope for. Finding deeper fulfillment in our partnerships comes from better alignment with ourselves and others, and from recognizing that not every relationship needs to meet every need. From our own experiences and reflections, we've come to appreciate the beauty of valuing who we get to be in each of our relationships, without needing every relationship to fulfill every role, or touch every part of our lives.

As you think about your own relationships, within Acro or otherwise, what have you noticed about how you tend to feel in your closest connections? *Do you feel like you can show up authentically without holding parts of yourself in reserve? Are there relationships where it feels like you're giving more than you're receiving? Do the people in your life offer you a sense of refuge, encouragement, and inspiration to explore who you are and what's possible?*

We've experienced a wide range of relationships throughout our time in Acro. Some have given us deep comfort and steadiness, especially during challenging times. Others have been a source of energy, excitement, and adventure. What we've come to appreciate is the diversity of what relationships can offer, and how freeing it is to stop expecting any single one to fulfill every part of us. Over the past decade, both Kate and I have been immersed in Acro communities around the world. While we haven't always had a single consistent partner, we've shared meaningful partnerships with many different people, each offering unique lessons and growth. Through these experiences, we've taken time to reflect on what contributes to the most fulfilling partnerships. Along the way, we've noticed strong parallels between healthy Acro dynamics and the ideas found in attachment theory. As we dove deeper into the framework of this theory, we discovered additional principles that not only made sense of our past experiences, but also aligned with what we'd seen in long-term, successful partnerships among acrobats.

Exploring attachment theory has been especially valuable in

helping us understand what supports or hinders the development of healthy Acro partnerships. At its core, attachment theory helps us make sense of how we connect to others, how we build trust, and how we respond to uncertainty or conflict, all of which are key elements in any Acro relationship. While Acro often appears to be about physical skill and communication, much of the experience is rooted in emotional safety, trust, and our responses to moments of uncertainty or vulnerability. The way we react when things go wrong, whether it's a failed skill, a moment of miscommunication, or a shift in commitment, often echoes the patterns we've developed in earlier relationships. By becoming more aware of our own attachment tendencies, we have learned to recognize when we're acting from old habits, when we need to ask for reassurance, or when we might need to offer it. Understanding these dynamics gives us tools to co-create more resilient, responsive, and mutually supportive partnerships, whether for a single session or over the course of years.

Other frameworks that enrich our understanding of healthy partnerships are the Sound Relationship House Theory and the work of psychologist Alexandra H. Solomon. These frameworks offer grounded, research-based insights into what makes relationships thrive over time. For instance, The Sound Relationship House emphasizes the importance of shared meaning, emotional trust, and intentional conflict management, skills that directly support the kind of connection, communication, and mutual care needed in both Acro and everyday relationships. Similarly, Solomon's work highlights relational self-awareness: the practice of understanding how our inner worlds shape the way we engage with others. In the context of Acro, this means recognizing how our communication patterns and personal boundaries show up in physical and emotional connection. Together, these perspectives offer us a means for not only building stronger personal relationships, but also for cultivating more connected, resilient, and supportive Acro communities.

In order to maintain an accurate review of the studies and their conclusions, this section may not specifically reference Acro relationships, but keep in mind that the concepts we explore here are still deeply connected to the practice of Acro and the way we build relationships in our communities. These ideas offer insight into how we show up for one another, how we form partnerships, and how we can move forward with more clarity and intention. In Part Three of this book, we'll return to these themes with a focus on how they apply more directly to Acro relationships and our wider lives.

4

Brief Overview of Attachment Theory

The feeling of attachment is an emotional and physical connection between two people that endures even when they are apart. Attachment often deepens over time and is a natural sensation that humans are wired to desire and need. We are born needing care and nourishment, and we innately expect our caregivers, our first attachment figures, to provide those things for us. John Bowlby, the initial author of attachment theory,[1] explains this phenomenon of innate human expectation for closeness as stemming from the *attachment behavioral system.* He states that it is one of several behavioral systems inherent to humans.

The attachment that can be seen in infants can give us an understanding of how attachment can also develop into adulthood. Some of the needs that infants expect and require are the physical and biological needs. These include caring touch and closeness, psychological security, and responsive emotional attunement. The behavior of infants changes when their attachment system is activated by fear, distress, or discomfort. In these states, infants reach out toward their attachment figures by crying, calling out, or physically moving toward their attachment figures. The infant's behaviors are attempts to find comfort and safety. If the infant receives the care, reassurance, or support from their caregiver that they need to restore a sense of safety, then their nervous systems return to a state of calm homeostasis, and their attachment system is rewarded and reinforced.

Infants and young children depend on caregivers for their well-being. They are not fully able to regulate their own emotional states so they must co-regulate with their caregivers. When infants are able to connect and be soothed by their caregivers, they learn over time to regulate their own emotional states, that is, **self soothe**. When an infant is able to know and feel that their attachment figures will be there for them in times of need, they will feel like they have a **safe haven** and **secure base**. These allow the infant to explore, knowing they can always return. John Bowlby explained this as the *exploratory behavioral system.*[2] It presents when attachment needs are being met and infants feel comfortable exploring for themselves, either toward other people or the world around them.

Depending on the responsiveness and feelings of connectedness that children have with their caregivers, they develop more secure or insecure styles of attachment. Based on the research by John Bowlby and Mary Aisworth,[34] in simplified terms, if caregivers are able to meet the needs of their children enough of the time, the children should be able to develop secure attachment styles.[5] In the other cases, where caregivers are inconsistent, unresponsive, or even dangerous, children may develop more insecure attachment styles. The ways that children develop attachment with their caregivers have a deep effect on the ways those children engage with other people and how they explore the world around them. We will dive into some of the ways that different attachment styles are described according to this research and more recent research studies.

One aspect of understanding attachment theory, when it comes to relationships and individual development, is that it is important and necessary to have healthy attachments to those who can and do care for each other. This is an innate human survival strategy that is developed early and persists through our entire lifetime. Our early attachment style is shaped by the environment we're born into and how well our caregivers are able to meet our emotional and developmental needs. Some of these conditions were within our parents' control, while others were not. When those needs are consistently met with care and attunement, we're more likely to develop a secure attachment style, where we feel safe both in the presence of our caregivers and in our independent exploration of the world.

However, when those needs are not reliably met, we may develop an insecure attachment style. This can manifest in different ways: by withdrawing inward and avoiding emotional closeness, by turning outward in an anxious attempt to seek constant reassurance, or by shifting between the two. These attachment styles develop based on our childhood experiences and continue to develop and impact how each person bonds and establishes attachment in their adult relationships, whether they are platonic, romantic, or emotionally intimate.

Secure Attachment

When children have responsive caregivers and a supportive environment in their early attachment experiences, they learn to regulate their own positive and negative emotional states. Early positive attachment experiences have a significant impact on healthy brain development and emotional regulation. These positive experiences of co-regulating with a caregiver help children to have lower stress hormones and increased oxytocin. Children who develop in this manner have an increasing ability to cope with stress and may learn empathy and social cues. In addition, these children may tend to have better self-esteem, stronger social skills, more resilience to trauma, and stronger overall emotional health. Reliable relationships with caregivers send repetitive signals to children that the world is a friendly place, they can ask for what they want, and knowing that the people in their lives care and will try to help.

As these children become adults, they tend to be more comfortable with personal autonomy and independence. They tend to form closer relationships. While they may miss their partners when apart, they are comfortable with themselves while they are alone. Compared to the insecure attachment styles, adults with a secure attachment style tend to feel less fear of abandonment when temporarily apart from their partners. They have the ability to trust their emotional bonds and maintain them during physical or emotional separation. During distress, these individuals can emotionally self-regulate their emotional states, while also co-regulating with their partners to receive support and reassurance.

Having a secure attachment with their partner allows a person to regulate their own emotions when distressed and also co-regulate with their partners to give and receive support. Partners who are embracing secure attachment styles often are able to take care of their own needs as well as communicate when they need help or assistance. Even though individuals may feel distress from feelings of separation or other outside factors, because they are embracing their attachments to their partners in a secure style means they don't have to act based on those feelings of distress. Recognizing that there are ways that their partners may be able to help them regulate their emotions and asking for that help shows healthy attachment, and reinforces those secure attachment bonds.

Communication from a secure attachment style tends to include healthy boundary setting and communication with consent. People in secure-attachment relationships often communicate openly and honestly. When those in relationship can be depended on to say no when they mean no, and yes when they mean yes, supports their safe reliance on each other. Each person can believe the other's consent when asking for what they need. We will cover more about healthy communication in later chapters.

The research by Kristen Mark et al.[6] has also shown that having a secure attachment style as an adult is correlated with higher levels of relationship satisfaction and balance, higher levels of empathy, respect and forgiveness for partners, and higher levels of sexual satisfaction when compared to people who are insecurely attached in their relationships.

When Attachment Needs Are Not Met

Other than the secure attachment style, there are ways that attachment is expressed insecurely. When the optimal environment for childhood development and feelings of safety are not available to a child, they may develop insecure attachment adaptations. Based on the research of Mary Main and Judith Solomon,[7] there are three expressions of insecure attachment: avoidant, anxious, and disorganized. Depending on what kind of attachment adaptations are adopted, children, and the adults they grow into, may struggle with certain relational skills or interactions. In developing one of the insecure attachment styles, a person usually has issues regulating their emotional states in healthy ways. As described in the research, these people may deactivate, suppress, or withdraw from their emotions. Or they may hyperactivate, inflame, or be easily taken over by their emotional states.

Children learn how to self-regulate their emotions through their connections with attachment figures. When children have parents or attachment figures that have trouble regulating their own emotions, it is unlikely they can support their children to develop a healthy self-regulation framework. There may be multiple reasons an attachment figure has trouble regulating, from being overwhelmed with stress, to being impacted by unresolved trauma. Children who grow up in environments leading to insecure attachment styles can internalize the beliefs that the world is unsafe and most people cannot truly be relied on.

When children don't have the opportunity to develop emotional regulation and soothing skills with the support of their parents, they often have to learn these challenging developmental tasks on their own later in life. One key skill that may have been affected is relational object constancy: the ability to trust that a bond or connection with someone will remain intact through temporary separations, disagreements, or emotional distance. Without a strong sense of this emotional steadiness, adult relationships can feel much more fragile. It becomes harder to cope with the natural ups and downs that come with closeness, like misunderstandings, conflict, or time apart. You might find yourself feeling panicked or deeply unsettled when a partner pulls away, even briefly. If this sounds familiar, know that it's not a personal failing. It simply means there's an area of growth from earlier in life that you now have a chance to revisit and strengthen.

Insecure Attachment Styles

In the traditional framework of attachment theory, there are three main types of insecure attachment styles, each reflecting different ways we may have adapted in response to early relational experiences, especially when our emotional needs weren't consistently met. The language used to describe these styles often shifts depending on whether the focus is childhood development or adult relationships. Terminology can also vary across researchers and theoretical models. Even so, the underlying patterns remain largely consistent.

The first two insecure styles are typically described based on how a person predominantly copes with emotional needs in close relationships. One tends to become overly focused on connection and approval. The other leans toward self-sufficiency and emotional distancing. The third includes aspects of both other styles along with disjointed other responses. Each of these patterns represents the way a nervous system has learned to adapt to its environment. Recognizing which of these patterns resonates with you can be an important first step in building more secure and fulfilling relationships.

It's common for people to have different attachment styles with each of their parents. For instance, you might feel very secure with one parent, but experience insecurity with the other. The level of security you feel in these relationships can be influenced by many different factors. It’s important to understand that attachment wounds aren't always the result of something the parent did wrong. Sometimes, disruptions in the attachment bond happen due to circumstances beyond the parent's control, such as physical or mental illness, hospitalizations, accidents, the needs of other family members, death, poverty, housing instability, war, or other social challenges. We will cover more aspects of this in The Nested Model of Attachment in Chapter 7.

Based on some of the research, adults with insecure attachment styles tend to have lower relationship satisfaction. While many of us in our developing years adapted coping mechanisms that are less attuned and more reactive, we still have the capability to figure out and improve the ways we self-soothe as healthy responses. In doing so as adults, we can develop mechanisms that lead to higher relational satisfaction. One such improvement comes from building emotional resilience and trust through the **continuity of connection**, but it can take time. The good news is, it's absolutely possible with self-awareness, practice, and supportive relationships. Instead of mistrusting partners, lashing out, shutting down, or pulling away in emotional reactivity, we can learn how to rely on others in healthy ways and figure out when it's appropriate to seek support from others to help us regulate our emotional states. Learning to trust and even forgive partners when facing challenges, responding with intention instead of reacting out of habit, and being willing to be vulnerable, will all lead to having overall higher relationship satisfaction.

Avoidant/Dismissive Attachment Style

Someone with an avoidant attachment style likely didn't receive the emotional support and attunement they needed from their caregivers early in life. As a result, they learned to survive by becoming self-reliant and minimizing their need for connection. This style may also be referred to as dismissive or dismissive-avoidant. When emotional nourishment is scarce or absent in childhood, it's understandable that a person might come to believe that relationships aren't a reliable source of comfort or safety. This often leads to difficulty being vulnerable, opening up, or trusting others with their inner world. To protect themselves from emotional pain, individuals with this attachment style may subconsciously push their own feelings and needs out of awareness. Over time, this creates a pattern of emotional disconnection, not just from others, but from themselves as well. Despite this disconnection, they may still feel a deep, often unspoken longing for closeness and intimacy. However, when opportunities for connection arise, they might not know how to bridge the emotional gap. This can lead to missed chances for meaningful support or closeness in relationships, both in giving and receiving care.

While the name may suggest otherwise, people with this attachment style do desire to be in relationships. The name comes from the tendency for people with this attachment style to struggle with reconciling their internal emotional responses. There tends to be a gap or barrier within a person with an avoidant attachment style that prevents introspection on the causes of emotional stress or pleasure. They have trouble responding to their partners in an attuned or sensitive manner as well. Feelings of vulnerability, and by extension intimacy, can be especially daunting to someone functioning with this style of attachment. When tough emotions come up, people with avoidant-attachment-style behaviors tend to ignore them, or distract themselves from dealing with those emotions. This can arise either by suppressing their connection to the emotions or distancing themselves from the triggers for those emotions. This can look like someone not willing to have hard discussions, or even needing to walk out of a room when conflict or difficult conversations come up.

If you resonate with the idea of needing space in relationships, struggling to express emotions, or feeling overwhelmed by emotional closeness, you might identify with an avoidant or dismissive attachment style. People with this style often learned early on that their emotional needs wouldn't be met consistently, so they adapted by becoming self-sufficient and emotionally reserved. Over time, this can lead to a habit of keeping others at a distance, especially during emotionally intense moments. You might find yourself downplaying your feelings, avoiding conflict, or pulling away when someone tries to get close, not because you don't care, but because vulnerability feels unfamiliar, or even unsafe.

People with an avoidant attachment style often lean more heavily on logical, linear thinking. They may find comfort and even success in areas of life where practical problem-solving and clear reasoning are valued, both professionally and personally. This strength in rational thinking, however, can sometimes come at the expense of emotional awareness. If you tend to rely more on logic than emotion and find it easier to focus on tasks than to navigate emotional conversations, you may have developed strengths in thinking clearly and solving problems, but sometimes feel disconnected from your own emotional experiences or needs. Maybe you find yourself in relationships but struggle to express your needs, dismissing them as unimportant. You might feel that desire show up in subtle ways, perhaps wishing someone would reach out, but are unsure how to respond when they do.

Embracing a more secure attachment style requires that you allow space for emotional experiences to emerge, even when they feel uncomfortable. This process involves tuning into your inner world and the emotional sensations that show up in your body and heart, not just the rational thought-based part of your mind. It's about learning to notice and sit with feelings instead of dismissing them. As you become more attuned to your own emotions, you also become more able to recognize and respond to the emotions of others. Over time, this can open the door to deeper vulnerability, trust, and connection. If you see yourself in these patterns, remember: it's not a flaw. It's simply an area for growth and one that you can absolutely work through with patience, support, and self-compassion.

Anxious/Preoccupied Attachment Style

People with an anxious attachment style, also referred to as a preoccupied attachment style, often grew up in environments where emotional support was inconsistent or unpredictable. As children, they may have experienced love and attention that came in waves, sometimes offered with warmth and care, and other times withheld or overshadowed by a caregiver's stress, distraction, or emotional unavailability. Because of this inconsistency, they learned to stay hyperaware of emotional shifts in people and work hard to keep connections intact. They demonstrate a hyperactive focus on their own emotional dialogue and have a continuous desire to resolve the many emotions that come up for them. Their nervous systems become finely tuned to detect any signs of disconnection or withdrawal, which can lead to a deep fear of abandonment and an ongoing need for reassurance.

A defining factor of the anxious attachment style is how the hyperactivated coping response amplifies attachment bids and intensifies the focus on partners. Someone with these attachment-style behaviors is often preoccupied by the connection with their attachment figure, prizing it over a reliance on themselves to satisfy their emotional needs. Their attachment system is overly sensitive to signals that their attachment figure may stop being able to care for them. They are constantly trying to keep their attachment figure disposed to care for them, or focused on them. For the person with this attachment style, this is, at its core, less about controlling their partner than it is changing their own behavior to get the emotional responses they need to satisfy their emotional needs. Their desire for closeness often comes from a deep internal need for the relationship to soothe their emotional discomfort and provide a steady source of security. In trying to hold on to that feeling, they might prioritize their partner's emotions over their own, believing that if their partner is happy and engaged, their own emotional needs will be met, too. This coping strategy can lead to overextending the self and trying to fix or manage the partner's emotional state just to feel close and safe. It's not at all about being "too much." It's a deeply human response to wanting connection and fearing abandonment.

If you often find yourself deeply focused on how close you feel to your partner and are constantly tuned in to how available or responsive they are, you might identify with traits of an anxious attachment style. People with this pattern of attachment often experience relationships with heightened emotional intensity. Small shifts in your partner's attention or behavior might feel significant or even threatening, out of a fear they might be pulling away or losing interest. You may find yourself reading into texts, tone of voice, or time spent apart, looking for reassurance that the connection is still intact. Over time, this hyperfocus on the other person leaves you continually disconnected from your own needs, preferences, and sense of self.

If you tend to move quickly in relationships, seeking early commitment or reassurance, this could be a reflection of that underlying attachment anxiety. You may find yourself swept up in the excitement of new love, interpreting emotional highs and intensity as signs of deep connection. This can lead to overlooking important questions, like whether the relationship is truly balanced, healthy, or mutually supportive. You might even find it hard to walk away, even after your partner has emotionally disengaged, or the relationship stops meeting your needs.

The focus of a person functioning from an anxious attachment style is on their partner. It most often leads to a loss of that person's own sense of self and ability to care for their own emotional, and sometimes physical, needs. They may become consumed by fears of abandonment and look to their partner, or to the relationship itself, as a source of identity and security. Partners of someone with an anxious attachment style may experience this constant monitoring of their responsiveness as controlling. They may also struggle to keep up with their partner's shifting emotional needs, which can deepen the sense of disconnection between them. Typically, people with an anxious attachment style have a history with unpredictable or inconsistent caregivers, and, by extension, have trouble trusting that their partners are reliable or will give their love unconditionally. They may even become self-critical of themselves and have self-doubt loops, feeding the thoughts that they may not be worth their partner showing them love. They may not be truly capable of receiving the full extent of the love their partners are already giving them.

Similar to people functioning from an avoidant/dismissive attachment style, people functioning from an anxious attachment style also have difficulty identifying and describing their own emotional states. Even though people with an anxious/preoccupied attachment style spend much more of their time and energy focused on emotions, by comparison, they have an awareness of both their feelings and their partner's. Where they have trouble is in differentiating the causes and sources of them. Although they are very aware of their partner's feelings, they are not necessarily reading them accurately. They may be very sensitive to detecting the slightest change in their partner's emotional state, but they are likely to assume the causes are personal to themselves and carry a sense of negativity, even when neither may be true. People functioning from an anxious attachment style often have trouble managing their emotional states, as well as trouble communicating their needs in an open and vulnerable way. The journey for people like this begins by embracing a more secure attachment style, which includes becoming more comfortable having time by themselves and not having to immediately respond to distressing emotions. They must learn to allow these emotions to sit until they can be addressed in healthy manners.

Disorganized/Fearful-Avoidant Attachment Style

The third attachment style is typically associated with childhood trauma, including neglect. The disorganized attachment style tends to develop when a child experiences their attachment figures as threatening, dangerous, or the source of many of their emotional distresses. The responses in this attachment style are demonstrated by a child who needs to distance themself from the emotional threat, yet turns to an attachment figure for safety and soothing. When the abuser and the protector are the same person, the child feels the need to both run away from and cower toward their attachment figure. The result is an internal collision of competing responses, making the child's own reactions feel unpredictable even to themselves.

As people with this attachment style become adults, the attachment style is referred to more often as fearful-avoidant. Such adults can have characteristics of either the avoidant or anxious attachment styles. People functioning from a fearful-avoidant attachment style may have simultaneous fears of being too close with their partners, or too distant. Because of their previous experiences with loved ones hurting them, they tend to feel uncomfortable, or fearful, relying on a partner, but may still have an intense desire for closeness with them. There may be reasons why they believe that speaking their feelings and needs could be dangerous, and they may be paralyzed by fear to do so when the occasion comes up. Their responses to a partner may feel internally conflicted, leading them to seek attention and reassurance while also recoiling once it begins. Even if their partner in adulthood is not causing new instances of reasonable threats, a person functioning from this attachment style may react to any feeling of closeness, or even their own behavior, with their awkward response patterns.

If you often feel torn between wanting closeness and fearing it, or are unsure of how to safely connect, you might identify with a disorganized or fearful-avoidant attachment style. As a result, you may find yourself stuck in a confusing cycle: craving deep connection, but pushing people away when things feel too vulnerable or uncertain. You might notice a strong desire for intimacy followed by sudden emotional shutdowns or withdrawal, especially when relationships feel intense or overwhelming. Trust may not come easily. It can feel like your nervous system is constantly on high alert. You may be unsure whether to move toward or pull away from others.

This inner push-pull dynamic can make relationships feel chaotic or unpredictable, not just for you but for the people close to you. You may struggle with regulating your emotions, or fear being hurt and abandoned even when there's no clear reason to feel that way. It's also common to have a hard time trusting your own instincts, wondering whether your feelings are too much, or if others will judge or leave you if you express them. Sometimes, even small misunderstandings can trigger intense reactions or fears of abandonment. People with disorganized attachment often struggle to feel emotionally safe in relationships, leading to challenges with regulating emotions, setting boundaries, or knowing how to respond to conflict. If you recognize these patterns in yourself, know that this style doesn't mean you're broken. It reflects the survival strategies your nervous system adopted in early relationships.

An important distinction in the research from Diane Heller is that this attachment style can be either a chronic primary attachment style, or a situational disorganized attachment style. In the case of a situational style, someone may function primarily from one of the other attachment styles, except in certain situations or when triggered. They can get activated into a temporarily disorganized, protective state until the trigger or situation resolves, when they return to their other primary attachment style. There could be many situations or triggers that activate this for a person, but getting past the emotional or psychological triggers is not something we will cover in this book. We recommend working through it with a licensed therapist.[9] Healing a disorganized attachment style involves developing emotional safety within yourself and gradually building trust with others through consistency, self-compassion, and support. It's a process that takes time, but it's entirely possible to shift toward greater stability and connection.

We have covered a lot of in-depth information about attachment styles in this chapter. To cap off this section, I shall point out several additional points to prepare you for the next chapters.

Viewing Attachment Needs as a Spectrum

Traditionally, researchers in attachment theory categorized attachment styles within one of the four types. In recent works, some researchers have proposed a better way to describe attachment by using two intersecting dimensions of attachment: anxiety and avoidance.[8] Creating a quadrant diagram with these as axes still places one attachment style in each quadrant, while allowing for more nuanced understandings, such as showing that not all people with the same attachment style have the same levels of avoidant or anxious tendencies. This visual model can be especially helpful in conceptualizing commonalities between categories while doing therapy or self-improvement.

Within the dimension of attachment anxiety, having a higher degree reflects greater fear of abandonment, rejection, or separation from an attachment figure. Individuals with high attachment anxiety may feel preoccupied with worries about their relationships and may seek frequent reassurance. On the lower end, a person tends to experience fewer of these fears and is more able to tolerate periods of distance or separation without significant distress.

Within the dimension of attachment avoidance, a large extent indicates greater discomfort with emotional closeness, vulnerability, or dependence on others. People in this range may prefer independence and often keep emotional distance in relationships. On the lower end, individuals generally feel more at ease with intimacy and connection, and are more comfortable both offering and receiving emotional support from their partners.

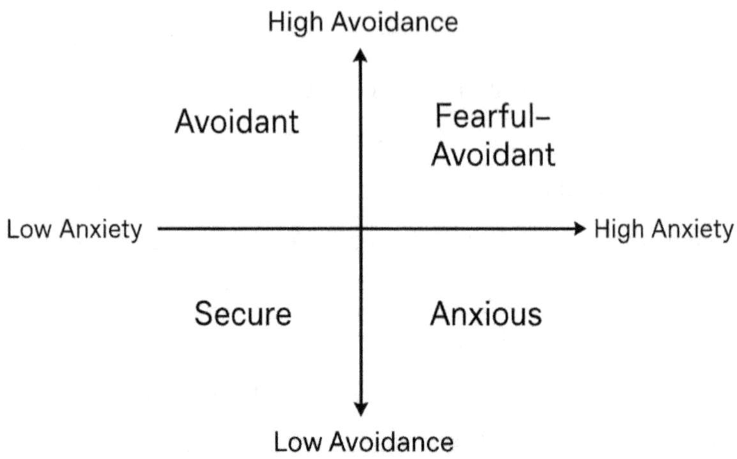

Two Attachment Dimensions (Levine & Heller, 2019)

Even within each of these dimensions, people may have very different experiences depending on the degree of attachment anxiety and attachment avoidance they carry. For instance, on the left are where secure attachment and avoidant attachment styles sit. They share low attachment anxiety. The difference is in how each person handles attachment avoidance. Low avoidance lends to a person being comfortable handling increased distance from a partner. Those with higher avoidance have more trouble embracing intimacy and being vulnerable. They may not even recognize or acknowledge their struggles with avoidance. Their low anxiety may be related more to repressing anxious feelings, rather than not having them at all.

In a similar vein, experiences for people with lower attachment avoidance, that is, those with secure or anxious attachment styles, may have little trouble reaching out to their partners for comfort. However, the difference in attachment anxiety may impact how intense those bids for affection may be, in addition to how they will respond when not reciprocated as desired. A person with lower attachment anxiety may approach their partner with a sense of openness, flexibility, and interdependence. In contrast, someone with higher attachment anxiety is more likely to seek proximity to their partner in order to grasp at or control them.

When we encounter having both high attachment anxiety and high attachment avoidance, there will likely be a high amount of reactivity to emotionally charged situations. Many times this becomes the fearful-avoidant attachment style. For those with a more situational response, they may normally be based in the quadrants to the bottom-right (anxious) or top-left (avoidant) until a situation or trigger increases their feelings of avoidance or anxiety. This would move their tendencies toward the top-right, fearful-avoidant quadrant. When they settle into a less reactive state of mind, they may return to the quadrant where they normally sit.

Our partners' attachment styles can significantly influence how our own attachment patterns show up in a relationship. For example, being with someone who tends to be emotionally distant or avoidant may trigger more anxious or preoccupied responses in us, while being with a highly anxious partner might lead us to withdraw or take on a more avoidant role in response. It's important to recognize that attachment styles are not fixed traits. They can shift over time. Both from one relationship to another and even within the course of a single relationship. These shifts depend on the patterns of interaction, levels of trust, and emotional safety that develop between partners.

Attachment styles are not rigid aspects of your personality or identity. The different insecure attachment styles do not define how you relate to every moment or every situation. It's crucial to avoid identifying solely with one aspect of an attachment style. It would not be fair to describe yourself as "I am avoidant" or "I am anxiously attached." Attachment styles are only one aspect of a person's entire identity. They help us understand how they behave. Conversely, we should avoid pigeonholeing our partners or labeling them based on their attachment styles, assuming that every behavior is a result of them being anxiously or avoidantly attached, or any other category in this book.

With any psychological model, it's important to remember that not everyone will fit neatly into the categories it presents. When a framework becomes too rigid, it can leave some people feeling unseen or misunderstood. Attachment theory offers valuable insights by highlighting recurring patterns in how people relate to others, and these categories can be incredibly helpful for self-understanding and growth. At the same time, it's essential to approach these descriptions with flexibility. Attachment patterns exist on a spectrum. The same style, like fearful-avoidant, can show up in milder, more moderate, or more intense forms depending on the person and their experiences. Holding space for nuance allows for a more compassionate and accurate view of ourselves and others.

As you explore these ideas, I encourage you to reflect on

your own attachment history. Consider the different styles you may have experienced with the key attachment figures in your life, such as parents, caregivers, or early mentors, and how those patterns may have shaped the ways you show up in your adult romantic relationships. This kind of reflection can be incredibly powerful and clarifying.

At the same time, it's important to hold these insights with gentleness and flexibility. While these frameworks can offer helpful insights, they aren't the full picture of who you are. While understanding attachment styles can offer useful language and frameworks, labels can also become limiting if we cling to them too tightly. Sometimes, identifying with a particular style or diagnosis can lead us to believe that this is who we are and limit our growth. It's easy to go from "I experience anxiety" to "I am my anxiety." As you read about different attachment styles, take what resonates, but try not to box yourself in. You are much more than any one label or struggle.

One final and very important point: having an attachment style is never an excuse for harmful behavior. I've heard people justify lashing out, shutting down, or treating others poorly by saying, "That's just my attachment style." But our patterns are not fixed. Please don't fall into this trap. If you notice yourself acting in ways that are hurtful to yourself or others, that's a sign to slow down, get curious, and seek support. Unhealed wounds deserve compassion, but so do the people around you. With the right help, cycles of harm and disconnection can absolutely be transformed.

Notes

1. *John Bowlby, Attachment and Loss, vol. 1, Attachment (New York: Basic Books, 1969).*
2. *John Bowlby, Attachment and Loss, vol. 2, Separation: Anxiety and Anger (New York: Basic Books, 1973).*
3. *Mary D. Ainsworth, "The Development of Infant Mother Attachment," in Review of Child Development Research, vol. 3, Child Development and Social Policy, ed. B. M. Caldwell and H. N. Ricciuti (Chicago: University of Chicago Press, 1973), 1–94.*
4. *Mary D. Ainsworth, Mary C. Blehar, Everett Waters, and Sally Wall, Patterns of Attachment: A Psychological Study of the Strange Situation (Hillsdale, NJ: Erlbaum, 1978).*
5. *Diane Poole Heller, The Power of Attachment: How to Create Deep and Lasting Intimate Relationships (Boulder, CO: Sounds True, 2019).*
6. *Kristen P. Mark, Lauren M. Vowels, and Sarah H. Murray, "The Impact of Attachment Style on Sexual Satisfaction and Sexual Desire in a Sexually Diverse Sample," Journal of Sex and Marital Therapy 44, no. 5 (2018): 450–58.*
7. *Mary Main and Judith Solomon, "Discovery of a New, Insecure-Disorganized/Disoriented Attachment Pattern," in Affective Development in Infancy, ed. M. Yogman and T. B. Brazelton (Norwood, NJ: Ablex, 1986), 95–124.*
8. *Amir Levine and Rachel Heller, Attached: The New Science of Adult Attachment*
9. *See Appendix for informational resources for considering therapy and other forms of support.*

5

Blending Attachment to Connection

Labeling ourselves, or receiving a diagnosis, can be useful in many ways. It can bring a sense of clarity and validation, helping us make sense of the challenges we've faced and offering a framework for understanding ourselves more deeply. Whether it's identifying with a personality type, a medical condition, a psychiatric diagnosis, or even an astrology chart, discovering language that resonates can feel like a relief. It can help us feel seen. At the same time, it's important to remember that we are always more than any label or struggle we face. When we look at attachment styles through the lens of attachment anxiety and avoidance, it's easy to fall into a deficit-based mindset, focusing only on what's "wrong" or what needs to be fixed.

Even secure attachment, the style many aspire toward, is often defined simply by what it lacks: low anxiety and low avoidance. But secure attachment is much more than that. It reflects strengths and skills, such as emotional resilience, relational flexibility, healthy interdependence, and the ability to navigate both closeness and autonomy with ease. It's helpful to reframe this. All of us, regardless of sex or gender, carry innate capacities for both connection and autonomy. These are not opposing forces, but essential parts of our human experience. When we understand attachment styles as different ways of navigating our core drives, we can begin to appreciate the strengths within each style, and work toward more integrated, balanced relationships without becoming overly fixated on labels or limitations.

Rather than viewing attachment styles solely through the lens of dysfunction, we can understand them through the values and desires they reflect. Each attachment pattern highlights what is most essential to a person, whether it's autonomy, connection, or a delicate balance between the two. By reframing insecure attachment styles, not as dysfunctional reactions, but as different ways of expressing our core human needs, we open the door to a more compassionate and constructive understanding of ourselves.

At the heart of attachment lie two universal desires, according to David Bakan[1]: the drive for **agency**, being in control of one's choices and maintaining independence, and the drive for **communion**, the longing for connection, closeness, and acceptance. These aren't opposing forces but parts of a continuum. Emotional health often comes from finding a flexible, responsive balance between the two. When we drift too far toward one extreme, we may find ourselves stuck in patterns that no longer serve us.

Take, for example, the avoidant attachment style. It is often described through minimizing or avoidant behaviors, but it can also reflect a deep alignment with the need for autonomy. In healthier expressions, individuals with this orientation may show strong capabilities in self-sufficiency, emotional regulation, and practical problem-solving. They are often skilled at navigating the external world and can remain composed under pressure. However, when pushed too far into self-reliance, this need for agency can morph into emotional detachment, isolation, and difficulty accepting support. The protective instinct to stay in control may begin to block authentic connection.

On the other hand, those with an anxious attachment style are often quick to notice shifts in emotional tone and are deeply attuned to the needs of others. When functioning in a healthy range, they can offer exceptional care, empathy, and relational intelligence. Their deep investment in connection can lead to rich, emotionally expressive bonds. But if that drive becomes overwhelming, it can spiral into enmeshment, where one loses touch with their own needs, boundaries, and sense of self. The desire for closeness may turn into overdependence, leading to anxiety and difficulty tolerating space or uncertainty in relationships.

By viewing attachment behaviors through the lens of the core human drives of agency and communion, we can begin to see how even reactive patterns stem from meaningful needs. The goal isn't to eliminate these tendencies, but to recognize and regulate them so they remain expressions of our values, rather than defenses against our fears. Secure relationships require us to "straddle" both of these drives, not as a compromise, but as a dynamic balance. With practice, we come to understand that autonomy and connection are not mutually exclusive. We can be both differentiated and emotionally close. In *Mating in Captivity,*[2] Esther Perel describes how too much closeness can lead to a loss of individuality, while too much distance can make genuine connection feel out of reach. She emphasizes that intimacy thrives when both connection and separateness are honored. Over time, we develop the capacity to ebb and flow between these states, navigating our relationships with greater flexibility, self-awareness, and grace. This is the skill of being able to use both reins, autonomy and connection, depending on what the moment calls for.

To build strong, resilient relationships, we must learn to honor both our autonomy and connection. Boundary setting is the key tool that helps us do just that. Boundaries are what allow us to remain connected to others without losing ourselves, and to stay rooted in our own autonomy without shutting others out. They help us clarify where we end and another person begins, which is essential for both healthy intimacy and self-respect. The balance between autonomy and connection is deeply intertwined with how well we're able to set, express, and honor boundaries. When our boundaries are unclear or unexpressed, we often feel the pain of misalignment, either from being too distant or too enmeshed. But when we learn to recognize and respond to our own needs for space, closeness, individuality, and mutual support, we begin to heal old attachment wounds and build secure, flexible, and mutually nourishing relationships.

Boundaries and the Giving and Receiving of Care

There may have been a time when being a good friend felt like always being available—answering late-night messages, canceling personal plans to help others, and saying "yes" even when it meant discomfort or exhaustion. Over time, this constant giving can lead to feelings of anxiety, burnout, and a sense of losing control. As we learn to navigate the many relationships in our lives, the skill of setting boundaries can mark a turning point in our friendships as we shift from transactional interactions to secure relating.[3] Boundaries aren't about pushing people away, but about creating clear guidelines for what is okay and what isn't. Limits we set on time, energy, and emotional availability, allow us to show up for others without losing ourselves. Our valued relationships won't suffer; they will grow stronger, building on mutual respect and authentic connection rather than silent sacrifice.

When it comes to our emotional needs and personal well-being, boundaries play a vital role in how we relate to others and care for ourselves. At their core, boundaries are the invisible lines that define where we end and someone else begins. Simply put, boundaries define us. They help us maintain a strong sense of self while navigating relationships. They allow us to connect with others without feeling overwhelmed, invaded, or lost in the process. According to the work by Alexandra H. Solomon, boundaries are how we establish agency, make choices that reflect our values and needs, and protect ourselves physically, mentally, and emotionally.

Healthy boundaries create a balance. They allow closeness

while preserving individuality. When we aren't able to maintain them, we may start to feel powerless, anxious, or disconnected from who we are. That's why learning to set and maintain boundaries is such an important part of personal growth and emotional health. They help us take ownership of our own feelings, responsibilities, and experiences. With good boundaries, we can "let the good in and keep the bad out."

There are many types of boundaries. The first and most basic is our skin. It physically contains and protects us, keeping essential things in and harmful things out. Similarly, we learn emotional boundaries through tools like language. One of the simplest boundary-setting tools we have is the word *no*. Being able to use that word confidently is a powerful act of self-respect, and it's a crucial step in setting healthy limits with others.

Navigating boundaries is one way to give and receive feelings of love and affection. Being with someone who respects and honors our boundaries can feel deeply loving and empowering; It creates a sense of safety and mutual respect that strengthens the relationship. On the other hand, when someone repeatedly disrespects or crosses our boundaries, it can feel unsettling, even chaotic, and often stirs up strong emotional reactions. These intense emotions can sometimes be misinterpreted as passion or love, when in reality, they may be signs of instability or emotional turmoil. Confusing emotional intensity with love can lead to unhealthy relationship patterns that are hard to break.

Experiencing disrespect for our boundaries in our formative development can create **attachment wounds**—disruptions in the ability to give or receive love from attachment figures. When a person is uncertain if they can express their needs and be listened to and acknowledged, it can make it difficult for them to give love when they are unsure that their love will be received. Fears of affections being rejected, ignored, or even taken for granted, can be paralyzing within a shaky relationship.

If we didn't receive consistent, safe, or respectful connection from our caregivers growing up, we might still desire connection with others, but find it difficult to fully accept. We may struggle to believe that affection is safe, genuine, and unconditional. That it won't come with strings attached or disappear when we need it most. Allowing ourselves to be truly vulnerable and let others into our deeper emotional spaces can feel intimidating, and sometimes we may not even allow ourselves to go there. It can feel unfamiliar or even frightening to truly let the people in our lives share love with us. But healing starts with acknowledging this fear and taking small, trusting steps toward allowing our connections to develop in our lives more fully.

Giving love can feel challenging when we carry attachment wounds. We may worry that our partners will truly receive it, whether it's enough, or if it will be rejected, taken for granted, or even exploited. We might fear that our love won't be reciprocated, leaving us standing alone in the relationship. Offering love, along with our desires for closeness and intimacy, is just as vulnerable as receiving it because, in giving, we expose our hearts and take the risk of being seen. It can also reveal our limitations, making it even more daunting. When attachment wounds are present, it can affect both how we give and receive love. We might find ourselves either taking too much or not enough from others, either over-giving or under-giving to our partners. These patterns often stem from boundary issues, where we struggle to find a healthy balance in how we engage with love and connection. By becoming more aware of these patterns, we can start to shift them, creating more balanced and fulfilling relationships. There are many ways that boundaries can shift and change that are directly related to keeping healthy relationships.

> *"My relationship with my mother has always had complicated dynamics that sometimes made it hard to connect. What made it harder is that we loved each other very much and were both committed to maintaining the relationship. As a child, I had no choice. My survival depended on staying with her. As an adult, I've learned more about boundaries and gained greater compassion for my mom's imperfect journey. At first, that process was rough. I didn't know how to set firm but kind boundaries, and she didn't know how to be un-enmeshed. She often said she wanted me to be her best friend, which left me parenting her emotionally more than a child should. At the same time, she justified restrictive decisions with "because I said so and I'm the mother." In my teens, I rebelled, snuck out, and did my own thing behind her back because her rules felt suffocating and illogical. She carried that expectation of authority into my adulthood, and it took a long time to*

dismantle. The relationship improved dramatically once she began to let go of those unequal power dynamics." J.S., Texas AcroYoga Community

Healthy Boundaries

Finding a sense of ease and flow in your life often depends on the boundaries you set and consistently uphold. Boundaries act as a foundation for your emotional well-being. They help you create space for your needs, values, and goals. When you're clear about what you will and won't accept, you're better able to move through life with a sense of stability and self-trust. This clarity not only supports your personal enjoyment, but also helps you engage in interactions without becoming overwhelmed or triggered. With healthy boundaries in place, you're more able to invite others into your life in ways that support your growth, rather than drain your energy. You can remain open to connection without losing your sense of self. When you find the right balance, pushing yourself to engage with the world, while also protecting yourself from harm, you're better equipped to navigate the ups and downs of relationships. Instead of being thrown off course, you can ride the waves, learning and growing through each experience, while staying rooted in your own center.

In the book *Loving Bravely*,[4] Alexandra H. Solomon defines healthy boundaries as the balancing point where you are able to both connect to another, and be separate from another, ensuring that you can maintain your own energy and sense of self while your partner maintains the energy that is theirs. Just like secure relationships rely on both autonomy and connection, maintaining healthy boundaries requires a blend of emotional openness and self-protection.

Boundaries are a form of personal protection, and it's our responsibility to uphold them. When someone doesn't respect a boundary we've set, it's up to us to take an action that reinforces that boundary, not out of punishment, but out of self-respect. This is the heart of what's called the **self-agency perspective**. For example, if being on time is important to you, you might let others know that if someone is more than 10 minutes late to a scheduled meeting or appointment, you'll move on with your day rather than continue to wait. That's not about punishing the other person. It's about honoring your own time and values. These kinds of boundary actions shift the focus away from blame and toward self-care. Instead of expecting others to uphold your boundaries for you, you're showing that you take your needs seriously and are willing to act in alignment with them.

When our boundaries become unbalanced, they tend to fall into one of two extremes: either too porous or too rigid. Porous boundaries happen when we are connected to others but not adequately protected. This is often exemplified by saying yes when we mean no, absorbing others' emotions, or losing touch with our own needs. On the other hand, rigid boundaries form when we protect ourselves so strongly that we disconnect emotionally, keep others at a distance, \avoid vulnerability, or struggle to trust. Healthy boundaries are not about being perfect; they're about staying aware of how much we're giving, receiving, and protecting ourselves. We must learn to adjust as needed to maintain both our sense of safety and connection.

Common boundary challenges often show up in a few key ways. One is **compliance**, which looks like saying “yes” to things that don’t feel right, or are even harmful. This usually stems from having unclear or fuzzy boundaries and a desire to avoid conflict. People who struggle here often minimize their own needs or differences just to keep the peace.

Another is **avoidance**, which shows up as saying no to good things. This might mean resisting support, avoiding help, or emotionally withdrawing even when connection is needed most. Often, this comes from fear of vulnerability or difficulty trusting others.

A third issue is **controlling**, which happens when someone doesn’t respect other people’s boundaries. They might take a no as a personal challenge or try to change others instead of accepting their limits. This usually points to a struggle with managing their own life or emotions, so they try to manage someone else’s instead.

Porous Boundaries

When our personal boundaries are too porous, it can leave us feeling emotionally drained, overwhelmed, or even unsure of who we truly are. This kind of imbalance often shows up in our relationships, both within ourselves and others, because we haven’t created a strong enough filter for what we take in or put out. Without clear boundaries, we may absorb the energy, emotions, and expectations of those around us. We may overextend ourselves in ways that go beyond what's healthy or sustainable. We might say yes when we really want to say no, or offer help when no one has asked for it, all in an effort to maintain connection or avoid discomfort. Over time, these patterns can erode our sense of identity and leave us feeling unappreciated, resentful, or depleted. Understanding the ways porous boundaries operate is a compassionate step toward reclaiming our sense of agency and cultivating more balanced, fulfilling connections.

According to Alexandra H. Solomon, when our boundaries are too porous, they can become unbalanced in two directions: taking in too much or giving out too much. When our boundaries are too open from the outside in, we are **absorbing**. This means we allow others' opinions, preferences, or judgments to override our own inner voice or better judgment. In these moments, we may feel underprotected because we haven't clearly defined where we end and someone else begins. We lose our grounding by becoming too connected at the expense of our own self-definition. On the flip side, when our boundaries are too open from the inside out, we can be **intruding**. This happens when we try to insert ourselves too much into others' lives or offer unsolicited advice. In other words, giving advice that wasn't asked for or trying to control someone's decisions in the name of "helping," is a form of intrusion. While it might come from a place of care, this kind of helping can feel overwhelming or misaligned for the other person, especially if it crosses boundaries they've already expressed.

In both absorbing and intruding, we often carry an

exaggerated sense of responsibility for others. Regardless of whether we're trying to fix, accommodate, please, or overcompensate, it usually stems from a boundary that needs strengthening in order to support healthier, more balanced relationships. Strengthening these boundaries can help us feel more grounded in our own values and emotions, rather than being swept up in others' needs or expectations. It also allows us to show up in relationships with greater clarity and authenticity. We can give and receive support without losing ourselves in the process. When we create clearer boundaries, we not only protect our energy and well-being, but we also foster mutual respect, reduce resentment, and create space for deeper, more sustainable connection.

Rigid Boundaries

When we develop rigid boundaries, it's often because we've learned, consciously or subconsciously, that staying emotionally protected feels safer than being vulnerable. These boundaries may form as a protective response to past experiences where vulnerability led to pain, disappointment, or rejection. While the intention is to avoid getting hurt, the result is often a sense of isolation or emotional disconnection. We may crave closeness but struggle to let others in, or we might find it difficult to express our needs, fears, or affection, even to those we care about most. Over time, this overreliance on self-protection can leave us feeling lonely, misunderstood, or emotionally stifled. Rigid boundaries might feel like safety in the moment, but they can subtly block the very connection and support we long for.

Rigid boundaries happen when we focus too much on protecting ourselves and don't allow enough connection with others. According to Alexandra H. Solomon, when our boundaries are rigid on the input side, we are **blocking**, and when they are too rigid on the output side, we are **restraining**. When our boundaries are rigid from the inside out, we block others from offering love, attention, feedback, or requests. We become overly protective and shut ourselves off from outside influence, often out of fear of getting hurt or attacked. This can make us appear defensive, prickly, withdrawn, or emotionally distant. On the other hand, when our boundaries are rigid on the output side, we restrain ourselves from expressing what is coming up for us, whether it's our feelings—positive or negative—thoughts, preferences, or even affection for others. We hold back, often because we feel unsafe expressing ourselves. We choose protection over connection. In either type of rigid boundary, we're leaning into our emotional protection, limiting the flow of love, and blocking expressions coming in or out.

Improving rigid boundaries can create space for the emotional connection and nourishment we deeply need, but may struggle to allow. When we soften these protective barriers, we invite others in and give ourselves permission to show up more fully and authentically. This doesn't mean abandoning self-protection, but rather learning to discern when and how to safely open up. Strengthening flexibility in our boundaries allows us to gently learn how to receive care, give love more freely, and engage in relationships with greater ease and trust. Ultimately, shifting away from rigid boundaries helps us move out of emotional isolation and toward more fulfilling, balanced, and reciprocal connections.

Boundaries and Self-Identity/Self-Worth

When we learn to trust ourselves by sticking to our boundaries, we can also learn to trust others as well. That's because when we stay true to our values, regardless of the situation, we can feel more comfortable opening up to others. It minimizes our fear of getting hurt. Another powerful result of having healthy boundaries is that we are no longer a victim of our circumstances. Instead we feel a sense of agency and confidence, knowing we can stand up for our needs in a healthy nonreactive way. In one of her talks, Brené Brown credits boundaries with allowing us to become actualized. She said that having secure boundaries "allows each of us to live within our integrity to become more generous and compassionate."[5]

Boundaries are rarely black and white. They're contextual, relational, and always evolving. One of the most important steps to feeling more calm and confident when setting boundaries is to remember that you are responsible for upholding them. It's not the other person's job to follow your boundaries. It's yours. From the self-agency boundary perspective, this means deciding in advance what action you'll take if a boundary isn't respected. This isn't about punishment or control; it's a premeditated, non-negotiable action that supports your well-being, and it's easy to communicate because it's about you, not them.

Sometimes, we only discover a boundary through

experience. You may not realize something makes you feel uncomfortable or unsafe until it happens. When that moment comes, it's a powerful opportunity to listen to your body and share honestly with your partner. Let them know this may be a new awareness for you. These conversations can become valuable moments of connection and mutual understanding. On the flip side, if someone tells you they don't feel their boundaries are being respected, it's important to pause and listen with openness. Rather than becoming defensive or placing blame, invite them to restate their boundary clearly so you can honor it. These vulnerable, honest exchanges build deeper trust and intimacy.

Reflect on moments in your relationships when you felt overextended, disregarded, or emotionally trampled. *Were these times when your partner ignored a clearly stated boundary, or were your needs left unspoken, leading to misunderstandings or unintended hurt?* Often, our boundaries remain unclear, not just to others, but to ourselves. When we take time to clarify our own limits internally, we become more capable of expressing them outwardly with calm presence and firmness. This clarity creates reliability and transparency in our relationships, helping others understand where we stand and what we need. Both of which are essential to building trust and meaningful connections.

Setting and communicating boundaries is not about creating distance; it's about creating the right conditions for true closeness. As Brené Brown reminds us,[6] "Vulnerability without boundaries is not vulnerability" Knowing when your boundaries are being crossed, and when you may be overstepping someone else's, is a skill that deepens emotional safety on both sides. If you've experienced hurt or betrayal in the past, it's natural to develop rigid or protective boundaries. That instinct to guard yourself is your nervous system doing its job to keep you safe. One of the intentions of this book is to gently guide you in softening those protective layers so you can stay connected to your inner clarity while building deeper, healthier relationships grounded in mutual respect and care.

Healthy boundary setting is a cornerstone of secure, lasting relationships. When each person can express their needs clearly and respectfully, they can build a foundation of mutual trust and emotional safety. In healthy relationships, partners learn to listen with curiosity and respond without defensiveness, creating space for each other's inner worlds. Boundaries help define where one person ends and the other begins, allowing both autonomy and intimacy to coexist. When we feel confident that our partner will honor our limits, and that we are willing to do the same, we become more open, less reactive, and better equipped to manage conflict with care. In this kind of relationship, disagreements don't erode the bond; they become opportunities for deeper understanding and connection. By setting and honoring boundaries with empathy and consistency, couples develop the kind of emotional reliability that supports long-term closeness and secure attachment relationships.

Notes

1. *David Bakan, The Duality of Human Existence: An Essay on Psychology and Religion (Chicago: Rand McNally, 1966).*
2. *Esther Perel, Mating in Captivity (New York: HarperCollins, 2006).*
3. *Mario Mikulincer, Varda Florian, Philip A. Cowan, and Carolyn Pape Cowan, "Attachment Security in Couple Relationships: A Systemic Model and Its Implications for Family Dynamics," Family Process 41, no. 3 (2002): 405–34.*
4. *Alexandra H. Solomon, Loving Bravely: 20 Lessons of Self-Discovery to Help You Get the Love You Want (Oakland, CA: New Harbinger, 2017).*
5. *Brené Brown, host, "Living BIG (Part 2 of 2 with A. B. Ruiz)," episode of Unlocking Us, January 4, 2023.*
6. *Brené Brown, Dare to Lead: Brave Work. Tough Conversations. Whole Hearts. (New York: Random House, 2018), 40.*

6

Relationship Frameworks to Improve Communication

In today's world, the way we relate to one another has changed significantly. The expectations we carry into relationships are often more complex and less defined than they were in more traditional societies. The roles associated with gender or identity have expanded, and while this has allowed greater freedom, it can also lead to confusion or misalignment when expectations go unspoken. Without clear communication, responsibilities can feel lopsided, and some areas of connection might be unintentionally neglected. With so many ways to define our relationships, it becomes even more important to pause and reflect on what we're hoping for, and how we want to show up.

In a healthy, supportive relationship, there's a profound sense of connection that allows us to feel truly seen and accepted for who we are. It's a space where we can let down our guard, knowing that our authentic selves will be met with understanding and care, including our flaws and quirks. In these relationships, we don't have to wear a mask or pretend to be someone we're not. Instead, we feel free to express our thoughts, fears, desires, and vulnerabilities, without fear of judgment. The safety we feel in these moments is rooted in mutual respect, trust, and a deep understanding that both partners are there to support each other's growth. When we can be our true selves, fully received by our partner, we experience the peace and confidence that comes from a sense of belonging. This sense of safety nurtures a stronger, more resilient bond that can weather life's challenges.

Building on the boundaries we establish for ourselves in our relationships, we can build trust within ourselves, and extend trust to the relationships we develop with others. When we take steps to be more reliable and stable, we can build deeper connections with the people in our lives, especially the ones closest to us. As stated by John and Julie Gottman, a researcher on relationships,[1] "Tiny little doses, every day, is what it takes to make a healthy relationship. Why? Because that's exactly what a relationship is; not one big thing, but a million tiny things, every day, for a lifetime" The ability to engage from a place of security and caring in the many interactions in our relationships gives us the space to create a relationship dynamic that fulfills our emotional needs and desires.

When partners feel free to be their full, unguarded selves and know they will be met with acceptance, the bond between them becomes a secure foundation for both individual and relational growth. By studying couples who have cultivated this kind of resilient, emotionally responsive connection, we gain a roadmap for how to nurture intimacy, navigate challenges, and sustain meaningful, supportive love over time. Examining the successful relationships identified in the Gottmans' research offers meaningful insight into the core elements that help committed partnerships flourish. These relationships show that emotional safety, trust, and genuine connection don't happen by chance. They are intentionally cultivated through consistent acts of care, empathy, and mutual respect in everyday interactions.

A Basis to Understand Relationship Success

We can learn a great deal about the relationships we want to build by observing long-standing relationships shaped by positive feelings and mutual care. Drs. John and Julie Gottman's research[2] shows us many of the elements and practices that contribute to healthy and fulfilling relationships. They have developed several frameworks for understanding beneficial relationship practices, with research studies to support their findings. We will dive into a couple of those that relate to secure attachment-based relationships.

To understand what strengthens relationships and supports their long-term stability, Drs. John and Julie Gottman developed the Sound Relationship House Theory,[1] a comprehensive, research-based framework that identifies the emotional and behavioral patterns foundational to healthy, committed partnerships. Rooted in decades of research, this model outlines the specific relational patterns that contribute to the development of secure emotional bonds. These are patterns that foster trust, intimacy, and resilience in relationships. In particular, the Gottmans' model emphasizes how partners can deepen their connection, manage conflict constructively, and create a shared sense of meaning and purpose. Their theory also illuminates the destructive dynamics that lead to emotional disengagement and undermine trust, often ending in relationship deterioration.

Central to this framework is an understanding of emotional attunement, or, the ability to be in sync with a partner's emotional needs and responses. Partners who engage in emotionally attuned interactions are better able to maintain a secure foundation within the relationship, which in turn facilitates greater interpersonal regulation. The Gottmans' research identifies the importance of managing physiological arousal during moments of conflict, as well as the need to avoid emotional states of hyperfixation or overwhelm, which can impede effective communication and emotional connection. These areas of emotional regulation are key to creating the conditions for healthy attachment dynamics, where each partner feels safe, supported, and understood.

To add further depth to aspects of relationship dynamics, the Gottman Relationship Method[3] provides valuable insights that can improve our understanding of relationships. This framework focuses on how couples communicate within relationships. At its heart, this method is about helping partners become better friends, manage conflict in healthy ways, and build a life of shared meaning and connection. This framework is a research-based model that translates theory into practice. It offers a clear explanation for why some relationships thrive while others become distressed with ongoing dissatisfaction, sometimes ending in divorce.

The Gottmans' findings point to two fundamental conclusions about successful relationships: First, partners consistently demonstrate care through behaviors that show respect, empathy, affection, and a general positive regard for each other. Second, they navigate conflict in ways that are gentle and positive, maintaining a high ratio of positive-to-negative interactions. This healthy ratio is essential for promoting a sense of emotional safety and security in the relationship, especially during times of tension.

As laid out, the Gottman Method is a research-informed framework built on systematic observation and outcome-based findings. Its interventions are designed to help couples enhance emotional engagement, communicate with intention and care, navigate conflict constructively, and co-create a meaningful life together. With these processes, partners can integrate relational skills with emotional insight to help them sustain secure and connected bonds.

Having curiosity about your partner

At the foundational level of the Sound Relationship House Theory is the concept of "Love Maps," a term coined by Drs. John and Julie Gottman[3] to describe the internal working knowledge each partner has about the other's world. A Love Map is essentially a mental blueprint that includes an understanding of your partner's inner emotional landscape: their values, dreams, worries, past experiences, sensitivities, and current stresses. It also includes practical details, such as their daily routines, major life goals, personal preferences, and even their evolving beliefs and emotional triggers. This concept closely relates to the process of attunement, wherein partners find familiarity with each other.

The concept of *Love Maps* is strongly supported by attachment-informed principles, though not always named as such. Just as a securely attached child thrives when their caregiver is attuned and responsive, adults in romantic relationships also thrive when they feel known and emotionally held. Attuning to a partner involves more than simply knowing facts about their life. It's an ongoing practice of emotional awareness and curiosity. By staying connected to your partner's thoughts, feelings, values, and daily experiences, you demonstrate responsiveness and care. This process builds not only emotional closeness but also a growing sense of confidence in truly understanding them. As your knowledge of their inner world deepens, so does your ability to support, empathize, and respond in ways that foster trust and strengthen the overall bond. This kind of attentiveness helps to create a secure emotional base, from which both individuals can confidently navigate personal challenges and relationship stressors.

Research conducted by Dr. John Gottman[3] found that couples who had rich, detailed Love Maps were 90% more likely to stay happily married compared to those who lacked this depth of knowledge. These couples were also more resilient in the face of external stressors and interpersonal conflict. Because they were already attuned to one another's emotional needs, values, and stress points, they could offer support more effectively and were less likely to misinterpret each other's behavior as threatening or dismissive during times of difficulty. The research shows that partners who maintain strong attunement are significantly better equipped to respond supportively during moments of stress, conflict, or transition. They are also more likely to notice subtle emotional shifts and respond to bids for connection, which are understated cues or requests for attention, affection, or support.

Building and maintaining attunement is not a one-time event; rather, it's a continuous process of curiosity, attentiveness, and empathy. The Gottmans' model encourages you to stay emotionally curious over time by actively updating your Love Map as your lives and circumstances evolve. When you or your partner don't develop or maintain detailed Love Maps, you become more vulnerable to emotional drift. A lack of curiosity or inattention to one another's internal worlds can result in a sense of being unseen or emotionally alone. This leads to an increase in relational distress and can even mimic the dynamics seen in insecure attachment patterns, where partners become either anxiously preoccupied or emotionally avoidant.

In recent years, findings from interpersonal neurobiology have added further support for the importance of emotional attunement. When we feel emotionally attuned to our partner, our brains release oxytocin, which we covered in Chapters 2 and 4. The consistent practice of building and maintaining attunement has not only psychological but also physiological benefits, enhancing a couple's ability to co-regulate emotionally and maintain relational stability.

Sharing Fondness and Appreciation

Understanding each other's inner emotional worlds is a core component to the health and longevity of a relationship, as are ongoing expressions of fondness and admiration. The Gottmans' research consistently demonstrates that when partners regularly notice and express appreciation for one another, it fosters emotional warmth and strengthens the relational bond. These gestures of appreciation, whether verbal, physical, or behavioral, are not simply pleasant exchanges; they are foundational actions that promote emotional security and mutual regard.[4]

Furthermore, expressing fondness and admiration, another key level in the Sound Relationship House Theory, is closely intertwined with Love Maps. When partners express appreciation for each other, it reinforces emotional safety and deepens their bond. Consistent admiration and gratitude reduce emotional defensiveness, elevate trust, and support a positive emotional climate in the relationship. Conversely, when admiration is absent or rare, partners can begin to feel neglected, undervalued, or emotionally disconnected, which are experiences that can mirror relational insecurity and trigger distress.

When you or your partner feels admired and appreciated, it can contribute to feeling more emotionally safe, seen, and valued in your relationship. This emotional security lends to resilience during times of stress or conflict. Conversely, when expressions of admiration become infrequent or absent, one or both of you may begin to feel taken for granted, emotionally unseen, or undervalued.

Over time, this can contribute to emotional disconnection, or even reactive patterns that mirror insecure relational patterns.

One of the most clinically significant outcomes associated with regular expressions of appreciation is the development of what the Gottmans refer to as a **positive perspective.**[3] This is a relational state where partners are inclined to interpret each other's behaviors and intentions with generosity, empathy, and trust. In relationships where a positive perspective dominates, partners are more likely to extend the benefit of the doubt, assume good intentions, and respond with patience during challenging moments. Even when conflict arises, they approach one another with more warmth, humor, and openness.

The absence of this positive perspective often marks the beginning of relational erosion. When partners no longer feel emotionally appreciated, they are more likely to interpret neutral or even well-intentioned actions through a perspective of negativity. This can give rise to defensiveness, criticism, and stonewalling; these are patterns that the research identifies as strong predictors of **relational instability**.[2]

A positive relational lens does not arise by chance. It is built incrementally through small, consistent moments of connection, similar to the responses to bids of connection. Compliments, expressions of gratitude, shared laughter, and simple acts of kindness accumulate and create a reservoir of goodwill. This emotional reserve enables couples to remain emotionally connected, even during periods of tension, making it easier to repair after conflict and return to a baseline of connection more quickly. In summary, fostering a positive relational perspective through consistent appreciation and fondness is both a protective factor and a pathway to deeper connection. It helps partners navigate the natural fluctuations of life together with more empathy and connection.

Creating a Shared Reality

Another essential component of the Sound Relationship House Theory is the creation of a *shared meaning*, which is a sense that the relationship has a deeper purpose rooted in mutual values, life dreams, and long-term goals. In emotionally connected relationships, partners don't just cooperate or coordinate logistics. They actively engage in conversations about what gives their lives meaning, how they define their roles in the relationship, and what kind of future they hope to build together. This process of co-creating meaning serves as a framework for emotional alignment, offering both partners a sense of belonging and shared purpose.

You can build a shared meaning by establishing rituals of connection, such as regular check-ins, traditions, or simple daily routines. These actions help you consistently reinforce your bond. These shared practices aren't about rigid routines, but rather about creating intentional moments of emotional connection that can anchor the relationship. You can also promote this shared reality by having discussions to clarify and honor each other's role in the relationship, whether or not those roles support one another emotionally, divide responsibilities, or nurture each other's personal growth. These shared rituals and clearly defined roles contribute to a relational cohesion that strengthens emotional stability, especially in times of stress or transition.

The Gottmans' research[3] found that couples in long-term, thriving relationships often shared a deep sense of alignment around core values and personal aspirations. Rather than competing or feeling threatened by each other's goals, these partners made space to explore and support one another's dreams, even when those dreams were different from their own. This emotional support fostered an environment where both individuals felt safe to grow and evolve, knowing their aspirations were not only acknowledged but also valued within the partnership.

These findings emphasize that emotional satisfaction in long-term relationships isn't just based on compatibility or conflict resolution, it's also deeply rooted in the shared narratives, or reality, partners construct about who they are together, what they stand for, and where they're going.

The Gottmans' longitudinal research[2] found that couples who reported high levels of satisfaction and long-term stability consistently shared a strong sense of meaning and purpose in their relationships. These couples were more likely to engage in rituals of connection and to clearly define their roles in ways that felt equitable and personally meaningful. By intentionally exploring their values and supporting each other's growth, they created a shared reality that enhanced not only stability and satisfaction within the relationship, but also a sense of meaning and depth. You can do this, too.

Being Responsive to Your Partner's Needs

The Gottman framework highlights the importance of turning toward each other's bids for connection as your relationship progresses. When partners respond to these bids with empathy and engagement, it enhances the sense of emotional security in the relationship, promoting a deeper, more stable bond. This responsiveness to emotional needs fosters trust and builds the foundation for more secure attachment patterns within the relationship.[5]

One of the core conclusions is that emotionally connected couples consistently maintain emotional engagement with one another. Partners in stable, satisfying relationships were found to remain responsive to each other's emotional needs, not only during major life events, but also in the subtle, everyday moments that shape emotional connection. These repeated bids for connection and their successful responses were linked to greater relationship satisfaction and emotional security.

Another essential component of this method is the cultivation of active listening and emotional validation. Partners who are able to reflect back one another's thoughts and feelings and offer validation, even during disagreements, are more likely to maintain emotional closeness and resolve issues collaboratively. Such validation fosters a sense of being seen and understood, which contributes to relational safety. In contrast, dismissing or minimizing emotional responses tend to reinforce conflict cycles and emotional disengagement. Over time, validative communication becomes less focused on establishing right or wrong and more centered on preserving the emotional connection and collaborative functioning of the relationship.

> *"I'm currently dealing with burnout from pole and Acro. It's been hard to give myself permission to take a break from the things I love most. Even though I received a lot of backlash for stepping away, I also received some of the most affirming support from my semi-consistent Acro partner, who simply said, 'I have been there.' That helped me feel less alone. The other most helpful words came from my pole coach, who said, 'I am with you.' That alone made me feel loved, heard, understood, and honestly, made me cry." – A.G., Miami Movement Community*

Conflict, although a natural and necessary aspect of healthy relationships, is difficult to discuss and often viewed negatively. The ability to navigate conflict constructively, without resorting to blame or emotional withdrawal, is a critical element of relationship success. Partners who manage conflict well remain emotionally regulated and can respond to each other with empathy and de-escalating-aroused emotional states. They avoid defensiveness and, instead, accept influence from one another. Such behaviors are crucial for repairing emotional ruptures and maintaining a sense of emotional safety within a relationship. A successful conflict-resolution process fosters trust-building and reinforces a couple's attachment security, as both partners know they can rely on each other even during times of tension.

Conflict is conceptualized not as inherently problematic but as a natural and even productive element of close relationships. The key distinction lies in how couples navigate it. Partners who remain emotionally regulated, employ gentle communication, and attempt repair during or after arguments are much more likely to preserve a sense of trust and relational health. The Gottman Method includes specific interventions, such as repair attempts, calming techniques, and structured processing of conflict, that help partners remain emotionally connected even in moments of disagreement.[6]

The ATTUNE Framework for Conflict

While there are many teachings within the Acro community about communication and problem-solving, such as non-violent communication,[7] using "I" statements instead of"you" statements, consent-based feedback, and others, a framework with similar values was developed within the Gottman Relationship Method.[3] Conveniently, the framework's mnemonic also aligns with other principles we explore throughout this book. The framework for navigating conflict is labeled "ATTUNE," which is where they state that conflict is caused by a lack of attunement between partners.[6]

The first component of ATTUNE, Awareness of Emotions, emphasizes the importance of being conscious of both your own emotional state and your partner's. Couples are encouraged to recognize emotional cues and be mindful of how their feelings impact their interactions. Emotional awareness allows partners to recognize when something needs attention before it escalates. It creates the foundation for emotional presence, ensuring that important cues aren't missed in day-to-day interactions. This awareness helps partners avoid miscommunication and fosters an environment where both individuals feel understood and respected.

The second component of ATTUNE is Turning Toward. This is the act of responding to bids for connection or emotional cues. These bids can be as simple as a question, a sigh, or a look. Turning toward means acknowledging the bid, however small, with attention or engagement. This principle focuses on the importance of responding to emotional cues rather than ignoring or dismissing them. When one partner expresses an emotion, turning toward that emotion involves acknowledging it and offering support or empathy. When partners consistently turn toward each other, they create a relational environment where each person feels emotionally seen and responded to.

Tolerance, the third component, involves accepting that emotions, both your own and your partner's, are valid, even when they're uncomfortable or different from your own. This does not require agreement, but rather the ability to stay present with differing emotional experiences. Tolerance prevents escalation by making space for a range of feelings without judgment or urgency to change them. It contributes to a sense of psychological safety in the relationship, where both partners know they won't be dismissed or invalidated.

The fourth component, Understanding, builds on tolerance by inviting curiosity about the other person's inner world. It involves listening with the intent to grasp not just the content of what is being said, but also the meaning and emotional context behind it.

Understanding is demonstrated when one partner reflects the other's emotional reality in a way that feels accurate and attuned. This kind of validation doesn't require fixing the problem. It's about demonstrating that the other person's experience makes sense from their perspective.

The fifth component, Non-Defensive Listening, encourages individuals to listen without becoming defensive when their partner shares concerns or criticisms. Non-defensive listening means setting aside the urge to protect oneself or rebut what's being said. It allows a partner to fully hear the other without becoming reactive. Defensive reactions often create a barrier to communication, preventing resolution and deepening emotional distance. By listening non-defensively, individuals can maintain an open, non-judgmental mindset, which helps foster a more trusting and empathetic dialogue.

Empathy, the sixth and final component, is about responding to a partner's emotions with genuine care and compassion. This principle encourages partners to put themselves in each other's shoes and try to experience their emotions. Empathy is the emotional resonance that follows from the other's perspective. It is a felt understanding that conveys, "I get it, and I'm here with you." Empathy strengthens the emotional bond between partners, making each feel seen and understood, which is essential for navigating conflicts and building long-term connections.

Additionally, nonverbal communication underscores the importance of nonverbal cues in emotional attunement. This includes body language, tone of voice, facial expressions, and other subtle gestures that convey emotional states. By being attuned to both verbal and nonverbal signals, couples can better understand each other's feelings and respond appropriately, ensuring that both partners feel emotionally connected even when words alone may not fully capture the intensity of their emotions.

Avoiding the Negative Indicators of Unhealthy Relationships

The Four Horsemen of the Apocalypse is a term coined by Drs. John and Julie Gottman[3] to describe four destructive communication behaviors that have been shown, through decades of relationship research, to strongly predict relational dissatisfaction and eventual breakdown, if left unaddressed. These four behaviors: *criticism, defensiveness, contempt*, and *stonewalling* represent escalating patterns of disconnection that interfere with emotional safety, mutual respect, and the ability to resolve conflict constructively.

Criticism occurs when complaints are framed as personal attacks, targeting a partner's character rather than a specific behavior. Rather than saying, "I'm feeling overwhelmed by the mess in the kitchen," a critical statement might be, "You're so lazy, you never clean up after yourself." This global approach to grievances erodes trust and often provokes defensiveness in return.

Defensiveness is a self-protective response that often emerges in reaction to perceived blame. While understandable, it communicates an unwillingness to consider the partner's perspective. Instead of promoting resolution, it tends to escalate tension by deflecting blame or minimizing concerns, which can leave the other partner feeling dismissed or invalidated.

Contempt, which research identifies as the most damaging of the four behaviors, includes sarcasm, eye-rolling, ridicule, name-calling, and expressions of moral superiority. Contempt communicates disrespect and emotional detachment. It is not only toxic to the relational dynamic, but also correlated with physical health deterioration in couples, likely due to the chronic stress it produces in the emotional system.

Stonewalling involves shutting down or withdrawing emotionally during conflict, often as a response to feeling overwhelmed or emotionally flooded. While it may appear to be an attempt to keep the peace, it effectively cuts off communication and can leave the other partner feeling abandoned, invisible, or unimportant.

The Gottmans' longitudinal studies have consistently shown that the presence and frequency of these four behaviors are predictive of relational instability and, in many cases, eventual separation or divorce. What's particularly important, however, is that these patterns are not fixed. When couples learn to recognize and address The Four Horsemen early, they can begin to interrupt these cycles and replace them with more adaptive, secure-functioning behaviors.

This approach aligns with what we know from affective neuroscience and attachment theory: emotional regulation, vulnerability, and repair are crucial for maintaining connection and psychological safety. In place of reactive behaviors, Gottman couples are guided toward patterns of mindful conflict engagement, which includes calming techniques, emotional attunement, and structured repair dialogues.

In essence, the goal is not to eliminate conflict, but to learn to engage it in a way that fosters intimacy, rather than eroding it. By addressing Gottman's Four Horsemen directly, and learning healthier responses, couples can significantly increase their emotional resilience and the overall stability of the relationship.

Take some time to reflect on the fulfillment you experience in the relationships in your life. When you consider your most meaningful connections, whether with a partner, close friends, family members, or others. *Do these relationships offer you a sense of emotional safety and space for open, honest communication? Do you feel seen and heard, and is there mutual understanding and support?* It's worthwhile to gently explore whether there are areas where communication or connection could be deepened. Even in strong relationships, there is often room for growth, increased clarity, or greater emotional closeness.

Having access to modern relationship frameworks is a valuable resource. These approaches offer practical insights that aren't confined to traditional roles, genders, or specific abilities. They're flexible, inclusive, and adaptable to a wide range of relational experiences. The beauty of these tools is that you don't have to implement everything at once. You can begin with small, manageable changes and build from there at a pace that respects the needs and readiness of everyone involved. Remember that relationships include multiple people with their own perspectives and agency. By sharing helpful ideas and frameworks with the people you care about, you invite them into a process of co-creating a dynamic that feels nourishing, supportive, and fulfilling for everyone. Growth in relationships doesn't happen all at once. It's a shared, ongoing journey.

Notes

1. *Gottman Institute's Editorial Team, "What Is the Sound Relationship House?" Gottman.com, November 30, 2020.*
2. *John M. Gottman, James Coan, Sybil Carrére, and Catherine Swanson, "Predicting Marital Happiness and Stability from Newlywed Interactions," Journal of Marriage and the Family 60, no. 1 (1998): 5–22.*
3. *John M. Gottman and Nan Silver, The Seven Principles for Making Marriage Work (New York: Three Rivers Press, 1999).*
4. *John Gottman and Julie Schwartz Gottman, The Love Prescription (New York: Random House, 2022).*
5. *John M. Gottman and Joan DeClaire, The Relationship Cure: A 5 Step Guide to Strengthening Your Marriage, Family, and Friendships (New York: Three Rivers Press, 2001).*
6. *Julie Schwartz Gottman and John Gottman, Fight Right: How Successful Couples Turn Conflict into Connection (New York: Harmony Books, 2024).*
7. *Marshall B. Rosenberg, Nonviolent Communication: A Language of Life (Encinitas, CA: PuddleDancer Press, 2003).*

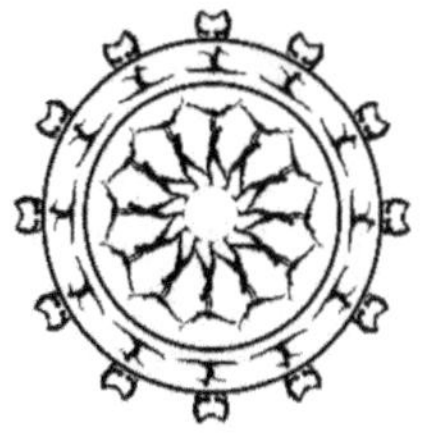

7

The Nested Model of Attachment Experiences

With the overview of attachment theory and some fundamentals of boundaries and relationship theories covered, we will now dive into another aspect of attachment: the impact of our experiences on our sense of self. In some of the work done by Jessica Fern,[1] a newer model of attachment and potential traumas pictured as nested layers. Her diagram of these layers shows levels of consideration for attachments to things that impact our feelings of affection. Fern's model supports the discussion of attachment principles and guidelines for relationships that will be laid out in Part Three of this book.

It's hard to explore attachment dynamics without also touching on trauma. Before we explore the different layers of attachment, it's important to first define what trauma is. We will be using the expanded definition of **trauma**,[2] meaning events that leave wounds with lasting impact on the physical body, psychological mind, or all-important spirit. In more recent decades, the psychological impact and treatment of trauma has been included in hundreds of studies. We have learned that the mental aspects of trauma can persist even after the physical body has healed from a wound. And as modern medicine now recognizes, trauma can also occur without a physical component. Traumas can result from single events, a series of events, or multiple sets of circumstances that cause physical, emotional, psychological, or spiritual harm.

Defining Trauma and Attachment Wounds

Traumatic events and circumstances can have a particularly strong impact during the early developmental years of a person's life. These traumas may stem from single incidents, such as assaults, accidents, or natural disasters, or from complex, ongoing, and often interpersonal experiences. They can significantly affect a person's fundamental sense of self and overall feeling of safety in the world. Wounds from trauma have the potential to disrupt healthy brain development, shape identity in harmful ways, and lower self-esteem.

Describing traumas has been done in many ways, one of which is that traumas involve situations that overwhelm a person's capacity to cope. Trauma occurs on a continuum of stress, and the difference between a distressing event and a traumatic experience is the body and mind's ability to recover from the experience. When a person is pushed beyond their capacity for too long, the longer-term effects of trauma begin to take hold. Left unaddressed, trauma can reduce psychological flexibility, impair everyday functioning, disrupt secure attachment, curb the ability to express affection, and limit a person's capacity for growth. If left unresolved for too long, it can have significantly negative effects on a person's physical, mental, emotional, and spiritual well-being.[3]

However, trauma does not affect everyone in the same way. Some people may carry visible signs of trauma, whether in their physical bodies or behavioral patterns. Others may bear internal wounds that, while not outwardly apparent, deeply influence how they perceive themselves and the world. Still, some individuals are able to process and recover from traumatic events without long-term harm. Each person's response to trauma is unique, shaped by a combination of their environment, support systems, and internal resilience.

When something stressful happens, our bodies naturally release a powerful mix of chemicals designed to activate the sympathetic nervous system, our built-in survival response. This response is meant to be temporary, helping us react quickly in dangerous situations. Ideally, once the threat passes, our bodies return to balance through the parasympathetic nervous system, allowing us to feel calm and think clearly again. However, in cases of intense or overwhelming trauma, this recovery process can get disrupted. The nervous system becomes flooded and dysregulated, unable to fully process the stress chemicals. This internal environment can leave us stuck in a heightened state of alert long after the event has passed.

Even when the stressors aren't dramatic or life-threatening, smaller, ongoing challenges, such as relationship strain, work pressure, chronic illness, parenting stress, or daily frustrations, can accumulate over time and have a serious impact. Instead of one big surge of survival chemicals, we receive many small doses throughout the day. If we don't give our bodies time to recover, we can end up living in a chronic state of stress, where the sympathetic nervous system remains overactive. In this state, even the perception of a threat can keep our bodies stuck in "survival mode," preventing us from accessing our natural ability to rest, recover, and thrive. Understanding this is essential as we look at the connection between trauma and attachment. These wounds don't just come from individual or relational experiences; they are also shaped by the larger world we live in. Cultural, systemic, and intergenerational traumas all play a role in shaping how safe, or unsafe, we feel in our bodies and relationships.

One of the newer definitions by trauma experts frames it as *the experience of broken connection*. Whether or not this is a broken connection with a loved one through death or divorce, a broken connection of the sense of safety in a certain environment or location, or a broken connection between physical body parts, these can all create prolonged signals of alarm or threat that our bodies must deal with. According to attachment theory, a broken connection with an attachment figure can mean death or harm for an infant or child. This is why feelings of separation from attachment figures can be traumatizing and, by extension, why different aspects of a person's experience, such as family dynamics, social expectations, or societal prejudices, can create feelings of separation from the people they are most attached to.

On the flip side of this, having secure attachments can be

helpful when dealing with trauma. A history of securely attached relationships gives one a protective buffer to traumatic situations. Research has shown that after a traumatic experience, people who are well-connected with others are more likely to recover more quickly and less likely to experience post-traumatic stress disorder, while people with disorganized interpersonal support systems are more likely to develop post-traumatic stress disorder.[4] Having multiple nurturing relationships help protect us when facing traumas outside of our attachment relationships.

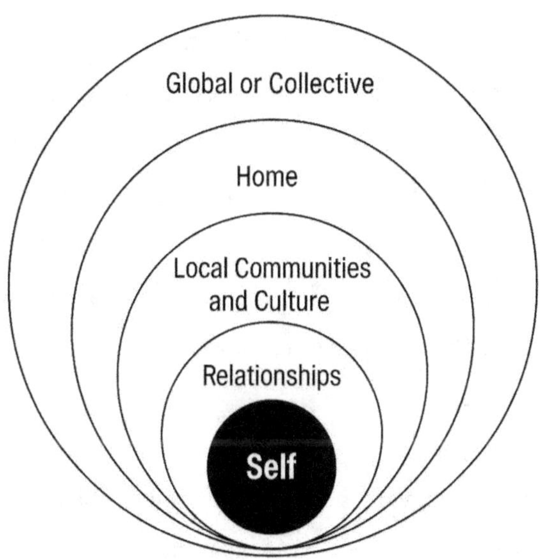

The Nested Model of Attachment and Trauma (Fern, 2020).

Self Level

At the very core of your experience is the individual self; it is the innermost circle that represents who you are at your deepest level. This includes your unique genetic makeup, the epigenetic influences passed down through generations, and the temperament you were born with. Over time, your personal history, including your early attachment experiences, shapes how you relate to yourself and the world. This self is made up not only of your thoughts, emotions, and self-perceptions, but also of how you interpret life around you. It includes the way you process experiences, make decisions, and learn new skills as you navigate the world. Your ability to care for yourself, to reflect on your actions and feelings, and recognize your needs and patterns all reside within this level.

The quality of your connection to yourself is foundational. It includes your internal sense of safety, worth, and centeredness. When this connection is strong, there's often a deep sense of inner calm and self-trust. When there's a rupture, such as from trauma, neglect, or overwhelming stress, your sense of identity and safety within yourself is disrupted. These inner wounds can make it hard to regulate your emotions, make decisions with confidence, or feel a sense of wholeness.

A key part of strengthening this internal foundation is understanding your values. Values are more than just a list of principles. They're a reflection of what matters most to you. They may shift in priority depending on your life stage, relationships, or roles, but together they form a compass for living with integrity. When you act in alignment with your core values, you experience a sense of authenticity and self-respect. As Tony Robbins says,[5] "The strongest force in the human personality is the need to stay consistent with how we define ourselves." Knowing your values helps you return to your center when life feels chaotic. They ground your choices in a deeper sense of meaning and truth. Cultivating this internal clarity is an essential step toward healing, growth, and secure relationships with others.

Relationship Level

The next circle outward from the self represents our interpersonal relationships. These are the connections we have with the people closest to us, including parents, family members, close friends, partnerships, and romantic or sexual partners. These relationships serve as the foundation of our attachment experiences. How we are treated by the people we love, and how we treat them in return, shapes the way we learn to give and receive love, how safe we feel in connection, and what we come to expect in close relationships. This is where the most direct and personal aspects of attachment theory come into play, especially in how we develop secure or insecure attachment patterns based on repeated interactions with these people.

The people in the relational level are deeply intertwined with the individual self. When a relationship is nurturing, emotionally responsive, and safe, it strengthens our sense of self. But when close relationships are marked by inconsistency, neglect, betrayal, or harm, those wounds ripple inward. Traumas that happen in the relationship circle, especially those involving people we trust, can be particularly damaging. These might include emotional or physical abuse, abandonment, domestic violence, or long-term neglect. Even when the trauma is not a single shocking event, but rather a slow erosion of trust over time, it can leave lasting marks on our nervous system, sense of identity, and capacity to connect with others.

Unfortunately, when we've been hurt at this level, it often impacts our ability to show up fully in other relationships, either new or existing. We might struggle to trust, to be emotionally vulnerable, or to believe we're worthy of consistent care. At the same time, our internal sense of self also shapes how we relate to others. If we feel secure and grounded within, we're more likely to engage with others from a place of authenticity and calm, rather than fear or defensiveness.

In Western cultures, romantic and parental relationships are often seen as the most central or "important" attachment bonds. This is reflected in research showing that many adults in Western societies rely primarily on romantic or sexual partners for attachment needs.[6] However, this perspective doesn't capture the full range of secure, meaningful relationships that can shape and support us. Close friendships, siblings, and chosen family members can all serve as viable, important attachment figures. In fact, some of the deepest attachment wounds come not from lovers or parents, but from trusted friends—when betrayal, ghosting, dishonesty, or unresolved conflict shatters the safety of those bonds. The death or loss of a close friend can also create a profound rupture in our emotional world.

No matter what kind of attachment wounds we've experienced, however, healing happens within our relationships. It's through repeated, attuned, and emotionally safe interactions with others that we begin to rebuild trust, restore connection, and reshape insecure attachment patterns. Whether it's through a partner, a close friend, a therapist, or a member of a chosen family, secure relationships offer the corrective experiences we need to repair old wounds. Even if our early attachment figures failed us, we are not locked into those patterns forever. Healing becomes possible through new, safe, and consistent relational experiences.

Home Level

The next layer of attachment bonds extends beyond one-on-one relationships and focuses on the broader family dynamic and physical home environment. This includes the structure, culture, and rhythm of life within the household during a person's formative years. Factors such as the number of people in the home, the presence of multiple generations, divorce or separation, growing up with a single parent, financial instability, or even periods of homelessness, can all influence a child's developing attachment style. These experiences may shape how safe, seen, and supported a person feels within the home, and, by extension, in the world.

The relationships with siblings, or the absence of them, also play a key role. Whether you grew up in a home where you had a close bond with siblings, had to compete for attention, or felt emotionally alone without peers to relate to, these dynamics leave lasting impressions. It matters whether multiple caregivers were responsive to your needs, or if the responsibilities of caring for a sick or disabled family member took priority. A sense of disconnection can also be shaped by grandparents or extended family whose values or cultural perspectives differ, especially when favoritism or relational misalignment is present.

Differences in personality, interests, or identity within the home can affect a child's sense of belonging. For example, being an introvert in a family of extraverts, having a different skin tone or neurotype than your relatives, or being an artist in a family that values science can subtly, or overtly, create a sense of "otherness." Living with stepparents or stepsiblings, or being part of a blended family, can add additional layers of complexity. Even elements like pets, whether they were a source of comfort or triggered allergies, affect household habits and routines that shape our emotional imprint of what "home" feels like.

While there have been many studies on attachment that focus on relationships with parents and romantic partners, sibling dynamics are an often-overlooked yet powerful influence. Many people carry deep attachment wounds tied to sibling relationships, whether due to direct mistreatment, or a lack of parental protection. Repeated teasing, competition, favoritism, or significant differences in age or personality, can lead to emotional injuries that echo well into adulthood.

The physical home environment also matters. Whether you had your own bedroom, or shared with someone you felt safe with, can significantly affect your sense of security. The energy of the home can influence the nervous system and shape a child's ability to self-regulate; was it too loud, too sterile, too cluttered, or too chaotic? Even relocations, such as moving houses or cities, can be traumatic or healing depending on the context and support. For some, home was a sanctuary. For others, it's a place they couldn't wait to leave. These associations influence how we view relationships as a whole: as permanent or fragile, abundant or scarce, safe or threatening.

When attachment wounds occur at the level of the home, they can manifest as shame or discomfort about one's family background or physical living space, which may lead to avoidant attachment patterns or difficulty with intimacy. However, by identifying, and processing, the most painful or triggering experiences from this layer, individuals can begin to heal. You can reframe the meaning of "home" in adulthood by intentionally creating a living environment and relationships that feel safe and supportive. These steps can restore a greater sense of trust and connection, both internally and interpersonally.

Local Communities and Culture Level

Beyond the home, our attachment experiences are shaped by the communities and cultures we participate in. This next layer of attachment includes the groups and environments where we spend our time, such as schools, workplaces, friends' homes, religious or spiritual centers, clubs, sports teams, or gyms. Each of these spaces represents a different culture with its own unspoken rules, expectations, and social norms. We may belong to several communities at once. Navigating their often contrasting values can be both enriching and challenging.

When we feel accepted and safe to be our authentic selves within these spaces, our sense of belonging grows, and, with it, our capacity to form secure attachments. However, when we feel we must hide, perform, or alter parts of ourselves in order to be accepted, it can lead to attachment insecurity and internalized shame. This disconnect between our true selves and how we are received in the communities we value, can wound our sense of identity. Over time, this may erode our confidence and strain our relationships at both the home and individual levels.

Attachment wounds at the community level often arise from relational trauma involving groups or authority figures. For example, being excluded from a peer group, ostracized by a clique, or subjected to ongoing bullying can deeply impact one's ability to feel safe and valued in group settings. Likewise, trust violations by mentors, teachers, clergy, community leaders, or individuals who serve as anchors in our communities, can leave lasting scars. When these relationships are damaged, it can diminish our ability to feel secure not only in that particular group, but also in future interpersonal and social environments.

In childhood, school is one of the most influential community environments. Children spend the majority of their time outside the home at school. The social and academic culture of that space plays a significant role in shaping attachment patterns. Positive school experiences, where a child feels heard, forms healthy peer connections, and overcomes challenges with the support of adults, can build resilience. Such experiences engender a healthy expectation that relationships are worth the effort they require. In contrast, environments characterized by confusion, rejection, or academic and social overwhelm can lead to withdrawal, insecurity, and fear of stepping beyond one's comfort zone.

A person's sense of safety in their neighborhood also matters. Feeling secure in public spaces, welcomed by neighbors, or embraced by the broader community, enhances our confidence to explore both our physical surroundings and our emotional needs. Conversely, experiences of neighborhood violence, discrimination, or traumatic events, such as school shootings or community unrest, can instill deep-seated fear and anxiety.

Despite the potential for trauma at this level, community settings can be powerful sources of healing and attachment repair. Positive peer relationships, friendships, spiritual or cultural groups, recovery communities, or even online spaces, can offer the emotional nourishment and relational safety that may be missing elsewhere. These environments provide opportunities to be seen, heard, and valued for who we truly are. They can foster the kind of connection that can restore trust in relationships and re-anchor our sense of belonging.

Social Level

As we reach the outer circles of The Nested Model of Attachment, we begin to examine the broader societal systems that shape our environments and influence our lives in significant and often subtle ways. These include the economic, legal, religious, medical, and political systems that define many of the conditions we live under. These span from access to resources, to social expectations, to the ways we are treated and recognized within our communities. This level of influence often operates in the background, yet it plays a powerful role in how we experience ourselves and others.

At this level, the impact of systems becomes deeply personal. The laws, norms, and institutional structures that surround us can either support our sense of stability and safety, or contribute to chronic stress and insecurity. A person's ability to access housing, healthcare, education, and employment is not only a practical concern, but it also plays a powerful role in how safe they feel in the world. When these systems do not meet a person's needs, or feel unresponsive, it can lead to a deep sense of disconnection, disempowerment, demoralization, or fear. This shapes their capacity to form and maintain relationships and to explore their identity, and life, with confidence.

There are times when the systems we depend on can feel impersonal or even unsafe. People may face barriers or restrictions simply because of how they live, who they love, or how their bodies or families function. For example, someone may find themselves unable to access the care they need due to the structure of the healthcare system. Others may face barriers in education, employment, or housing that create chronic instability and erode their ability to plan for the future or care for their families. In moments like these, it becomes difficult to feel truly at ease in the world. Over time, this can shape how a person engages in relationships, how they perceive their own value, and whether they believe they can ask for help, or expect to be met with understanding.

When these systemic stressors are ongoing, they can lead to what sociologist Johan Galtung called **structural violence,**[7] a type of harm that isn't always visible or direct, but is built into the systems around us. Structural violence refers to the gap between what a person could potentially experience in a supportive world, and what they actually experience due to the limitations created by these broader structures. This kind of stress can accumulate over time to create a sense of disconnection, helplessness, or chronic anxiety about one's place in society.

These experiences of limitation and invisibility can take a toll on how someone relates to others, to their community, and even to themselves. When the world around us feels unpredictable or unwelcoming, it's common to withdraw, shut down emotionally, or feel like one has to hide important parts of who they are. This disconnection doesn't always originate in individual relationships. It can be rooted in how society itself is structured, and how safe or unsafe that structure feels on a daily basis.

Even so, healing is possible at this level, just as it is within more personal spheres. Finding spaces where one feels seen, heard, and valued can begin to repair the damage done by systemic invalidation. Repair may come through art, activism, community care, or shared cultural expression. When people are supported by institutions that treat them with fairness, dignity, and compassion, it becomes easier to rebuild trust in the world, and to develop a secure sense of belonging. Over time, participating in, or even just witnessing efforts to build more compassionate, responsive, and human-centered systems can also help renew a person's hope and sense of belonging.

By understanding how societal structures shape attachment and trauma, we are better equipped to navigate our lives with gentleness and insight. Just as we seek safety and trust in our closest relationships, we also need to feel that the broader world we live in supports our efforts to grow, connect, and thrive. This outer circle reminds us that healing is not only personal, it is also shaped by the environments and systems we are part of, and by the shared work of building spaces where everyone can feel seen, safe, and supported.[8]

Global or Collective Level

The outermost layer of the nested model reflects the global sphere: our connection to humanity as a whole and to the natural world we all inhabit. This level expands far beyond personal experiences, relationships, communities, and even societal structures. It invites us to consider how global events, collective histories, environmental shifts, and the interconnectedness of life on Earth shape our internal world, often in ways we may not immediately recognize.

One vital aspect of this level is collective trauma. Unlike personal trauma, which affects an individual directly, **collective trauma** is experienced by groups, communities, or entire societies.[2] It can stem from large-scale events such as war, slavery, colonization, genocide, pogroms, forced displacement, famine, or systemic suppression. While individuals are deeply affected by these experiences in their own lives, the impact of such trauma does not end with the initial generation of people who experienced it. It continues to echo through families, cultures, and societies in both visible and invisible ways.

Emerging fields of study, such as epigenetics, support the idea that trauma can even be passed biologically. When large-scale traumatic events go unresolved, they may leave marks, not just in cultural memory or social institutions, but also in how genes are expressed across generations. These inherited changes can affect emotional resilience, physical health, and a person's baseline level of alertness to danger, further shaping their sense of safety, attachment, and capacity for trust.

At the global level, the relationship between humans and the earth becomes central. The health of the natural world is intimately tied to our emotional and psychological well-being, whether we are consciously aware of that link or not. For some, the state of the environment, with rising temperatures, polluted air, shrinking forests, and endangered species, is a source of quiet unease. For others, it is a source of daily distress, grief, or urgent activism. This relationship with nature is not merely symbolic; it is lived, felt, and embodied.

Even when our connection to nature is not at the front of our mind, the impacts of environmental change can still weigh heavily. Climate events like wildfires, hurricanes, floods, earthquakes, pandemics, and other large-scale natural disasters have become more frequent and intense. These events can cause immediate trauma through loss of life, home, or livelihood. Beyond the immediate danger, the aftermath can bring further trauma when aid is delayed, inaccessible, or unevenly distributed. People affected by such disasters often face long-term challenges in rebuilding not just their homes, but also their sense of security and stability. But even those not directly affected may experience what's now being recognized as **climate-related trauma**: a sense of grief, helplessness, or anxiety about the degradation of the planet and an uncertainty about the future.

Despite the scale of these challenges, it is important to remember that the global level can also be a source of connection and healing. Just as collective trauma can be transmitted through generations, so too can collective wisdom, resilience, and compassion. Many people find strength through community action, environmental stewardship, storytelling, and reconnecting with nature. Across the globe, people are working to restore broken systems, preserve cultural memory, care for the planet, and foster a sense of global citizenship. Communities coming together to grieve, reflect, create, and act, are part of a larger healing process that honors both the pain and the possibility of our shared existence.

Ultimately, this layer of the model reminds us that we are not just individuals navigating isolated lives. We are part of a living, breathing, interconnected world. By exploring our relationship with humanity as a whole and the Earth we all share, we can begin to process and respond to the traumas of the collective. In doing so, we build not only a more integrated sense of self, but also contribute to a more compassionate, sustainable, and healing future for all.

Trauma and attachment wounds can make it difficult for people to feel safe and secure. When left unaddressed, these can create significant impairment in a person's ability to connect with others, or even function healthily. The wounds that occur at any level of the nested-model of attachment experiences signal threats, cause ruptures, or damage trust for a person's attachment system. This affects how safe each person feels in their body, with others, and in the wider world.

How each person and their nervous system reacts to incidents and circumstances of trauma can vary greatly. Some people may hold traumatic incidents in their body for long periods of time, and others may be able to recover quickly from the same incident, even with the same support systems and similar attachment histories. The various levels of attachment do not have inherently more or less impact on people's systems as a whole, but each level can be examined to see where wounds have occurred, and what kinds of healing can be helpful. At each separate level, we can look at potential trauma and see how it permeates to the levels above and below. Although traumas that occur at the cultural, societal, and global levels cannot be healed entirely by an individual, repair that allows a person to more healthily move forward can be carried out at the self and relationship levels.

Healing is available to us at every level of our experience. When a rupture or wound occurs in one area, we can direct our attention and care toward healing at that specific level. At the same time, it's important to draw support from the other levels of our lives. Each one offers its own form of repair and renewal. Healing might look like practicing self-compassion, receiving a comforting hug from someone we trust, feeling at ease in a peaceful home, being seen and welcomed in a community, gaining access to rights or services that affirm our dignity, or simply taking a quiet walk in nature to restore our sense of balance. Healing is rarely linear, and it often unfolds through a network of small but meaningful moments across all these layers.

Notes

1. *Jessica Fern, Polysecure: Attachment, Trauma and Consensual Nonmonogamy (Portland, OR: Thorntree Press, 2020).*
2. *Thomas Hübl and Julie Jordan Avritt, "Toward the Integration of Collective Trauma in a Time of Exponential Change," Spanda Journal 7, no. 1 (2017): 75–84.*
3. *Thomas Hübl and Lori Shridhare, "What Collective Trauma Feels Like," Psychology Today, March 5, 2025.*
4. *Stephen Joseph, "Growth Following Adversity: Positive Psychological Perspectives on Posttraumatic Stress," Psihologijske Teme 18, no. 2 (2009): 335–44.*
5. *Tony Robbins, "#DateWithDestiny2025," Facebook video, December 5, 2025.*

6. *Cindy Hazan and Phillip Shaver, "Romantic Love Conceptualized as an Attachment Process," Journal of Personality and Social Psychology 52, no. 3 (1987): 511–24; Debra Zeifman and Cindy Hazan, "Pair Bonds as Attachments: Reevaluating the Evidence," in Handbook of Attachment: Theory, Research, and Clinical Applications, 3rd ed., ed. Jude Cassidy and Phillip R. Shaver (New York: Guilford Press, 2018), 416–34.*
7. *Johan Galtung, "Violence, Peace, and Peace Research," Journal of Peace Research 6, no. 3 (1969): 167–91.*
8. *Marianna Pogosyan, "How We Help Each Other Heal: Much of Our Healing Can Take Place in Relation to Others," Psychology Today, April 4, 2024.*

Part III

With more than a decade of Acro practice behind each of us, we have developed a deep foundation in both acrobatic skills and physical healing techniques. Over the years, we have also had the privilege of sharing what we've learned with others through classes, retreats, and private coaching. While we've deeply enjoyed the peaks of the journey, we are equally grateful for the lows, which have helped us grow into more aligned and authentic versions of ourselves. What stands out most to us, beyond the challenge and excitement of learning new skills, are the meaningful moments of connection. Specifically, these happen when we're able to drop into the moment and let our true selves be seen by the people we value. These moments wouldn't have been possible without the relationships we have built and the relationship skills we've developed along the way.

We have been fortunate to travel to a wide range of communities and countries. We've had the opportunity to train and connect with accomplished performers and teachers. In addition to learning their techniques, we've been especially curious about the mindsets that helped them achieve their goals and build fulfilling partnerships. Unsurprisingly, one common theme we've observed is the importance they place on finding and nurturing an Acro partnership rooted in shared goals that can grow with them. We have each taken these insights and applied them to our own practices, seeing firsthand the positive impact they can have. Of course, we've also had our share of missteps along the way, but those moments have contributed to our growth and wisdom. In this part of the book, we will be sharing the top lessons from our experiences, along with the wisdom from others' long-time partnerships.

In Part Two of the book, we explored various research frameworks and studies that support the principles we will be sharing, demonstrating that they have a strong scientific foundation and can be replicated to create positive outcomes in other relationships. Now, we'll shift our focus to how these principles can be practically applied. You can use them within your Acro partnerships, as well as in other areas of your life. When practiced intentionally, they can support the development of fulfilling connections that not only enhance your personal experience but also help cultivate stronger, more connected Acro communities.

Throughout our journeys in Acro, some of the most heartbreaking moments have been witnessing enthusiastic practitioners step away from the community due to unhealthy relationships, or the lack of a sense of belonging. In many of these cases, greater awareness might have prevented the situations. Whether it was a partnership falling apart because of miscommunication, someone stepping back from their practice to preserve a relationship outside of Acro, or a person feeling excluded or discouraged from playing as often as they'd like, these experiences often resulted from relational dynamics, rather than a lack of interest or ability. By nurturing stronger relationship skills, both individually and within our communities, we could have helped these individuals remain part of the community, enriching the experience for everyone.

As you read this, you may already be reflecting on your own journey with Acro partnerships. It may be that a partnership brought you deep joy and connection, or challenged you in unexpected ways, or left you feeling confused, hurt, or disconnected. Perhaps you've experienced the magic of being fully in sync with a partner, or the frustration of misalignment despite shared effort. Maybe you've found it difficult to express your needs, navigate jealousy, or balance your Acro relationships with other aspects of your life. If any of this resonates, know that you're not alone. These ups and downs are a natural part of partnering closely with others, especially in a practice as physically and emotionally intimate as Acro. They simply reflect the complexity and depth that comes with engaging in meaningful, intimate partnerships. Whatever your journey has looked like, we invite you to reflect on your own experiences as you move through this part of the book and consider how these principles might support you in creating partnerships that are not only more skillful, but more resilient, compassionate, and fulfilling.

The principles in this section of the book are organized around the different phases and focuses of an Acro partnership starting from the early moments of establishing a meaningful connection to building a strong, fulfilling partnership with a healthy foundation. We will offer insights and practices to support you in showing up more fully for yourself, your partner, and the relationship, with greater alignment between your values and intentions. Throughout the chapters, you'll find strategies for navigating the inevitable challenges and hard moments that arise, including a chapter centered on some of the more difficult situations people may encounter. While these insights are shared through the lens of Acro partnerships, all of these principles and strategies can also be applied toward any activity involving close partnership or teamwork between two people, and can be applied to romantic relationships as well.

8

The Foundations of Being AcroSecure

One of the most rewarding parts of doing Acro are the connections that you're able to feel with the people that you are playing with. There is so much extra information and so many sensations that you can feel when you are in physical contact with a person who is trusting you with their physical well-being. When each person is putting their weight into the points of physical connection with the intention of finding alignment, there are numerous micro-adjustments being made, both consciously and subconsciously. These adjustments range from how much pressure to put into the grip and whether to lean toward them or trust falling away from them, to even where you focus your attention. All of these adjustments are being continually processed and interpreted. The environment during Acro sessions creates a space where you can meet another person where they are, bring yourself and your experiences into the interaction, and form a connection that is truly unique. Navigating these interactions happens quickly and you can observe how your spoken and unspoken communication is interpreted in the ways that a person's body moves and reacts.

As you build an awareness of how you contribute to each interaction in the relationships you value, you gain more agency in creating the outcomes you want. The wonderful part of all this happening during Acro is that you often get to see the outcome of the changes you make shortly after trying them. This feedback loop can enable a significant amount of learning in a short period of time. When practicing in an environment where each person feels safe, it can allow someone to attempt things that would normally be outside their comfort zone, or even their perceived realm of possibility.

The ways people respond to one another in an Acro session share many similarities with the relational dynamics described in attachment theory. Cultivating healthy and supportive dynamics in our Acro relationships can teach us how to foster healthier relationships in the other areas of our lives. Bring yourself into your relationships and interactions more fully by developing the tools you need to communicate. Invite others into your personal space. Become aware of your own needs and desires, and collaborate in ways that strengthen the connections with each person involved.

> *"Acro partners are just like any other relationship you encounter. Nothing is perfect but communication and trust are key." –C.J., Acro Community Leader*

Do We Want to Be Attachment-Based Partners?

One of the prerequisites to being AcroSecure partners is first to come to a decision and then agree on whether or not you want to be attachment-based partners for each other. An attachment-based relationship takes time and investment to build in a healthy manner. When we speak of AcroSecure partnerships in this part of the book, we refer to partners who have intentionally consented and agreed to being emotionally attached to one another. Although most of the exercises in this part of the book are directed to attached partners, they can still be utilized by non-attached partners to improve their relationship and bonds, in that both people should be aware of the expectations and agreements they have with each other.

In many romantic relationships, aspects of establishing attachment consent are assumed when two people "define the relationship," or have a commitment conversation, but often there are a lot of assumptions in what each person considers a "committed relationship." Each person's hopes and expectations for the relationship are more fully understood when they are openly articulated, including whether being an attachment figure is appropriate and mutual.

Attachment-based relationships are not limited to your romantic partners. They can continue to be with your parents, siblings, close friends, or other consistent relationships in your life. Outside of your parent-child relationships, healthy attachment-based, secure relationships should be consented to by both people in the relationship, including siblings. Many times, people "fall" into attachment-based relationships and develop feelings and emotions based on that attachment, without an expressed, reliable agreement from the other person. It is important to communicate that an attachment is building with a person. This allows them to express their consent or exclusion to the implied responsibility of that attachment and minimizes the potential for abuse of the attachment. There are a lot of feelings and emotions that can be exposed when an attachment is formed, and there are many ways that a person can unintentionally inflict pain and hurt when they are not aware of their impact on that attachment bond.

One of the core values within the Acro community is *enthusiastic consent.* Safety and confidence begin with making sure each person understands and agrees to the movements or interactions that are about to take place. Consent communication means clearly and freely agreeing to participate in a specific interaction, with as much relevant information as possible. Consent is tied to what has actually been described, not to what one person assumes might also be welcome.

The tea-and-consent example[1] illustrates this clearly: if you offer someone tea and they say yes, you can give them tea. If they say no, hesitate, seem uncertain, change their mind, or are unable to respond, you don't pressure them or decide that they probably want it anyway. You also would not hand them tea and then add extra ingredients they never agreed to simply because you think they would enjoy it. In the same way, agreeing to one Acro movement does not automatically mean agreeing to a more advanced variation, a different kind of touch, or a longer interaction.

Enthusiastic consent goes a step further by recognizing only a clear, wholehearted "yes" as agreement, while understanding that a hesitant "okay" or "I guess" does not reflect full willingness. Its purpose is to ensure that everyone involved is offering genuine, willing consent. In a practice that can involve real vulnerability and physical risk, this helps foster a culture of trust, clarity, and care.

If and when both people decide to be attachment-based partners, you should be aware and willing to show up for each other regularly; prioritize each other to a significant level, from choice rather than obligation; actively cherish and celebrate each other; do the work to build the relationship and the connection together; and be willing to step into, and work through, the sometimes uncomfortable situations with each other.

Communication and Shared Understanding

Acro heightens awareness of nonverbal communication in ways that extend beyond what most people encounter in everyday life. The tone of voice you use when asking to play, asking for adjustments, or sharing feedback, can affect how well the other person responds. This can affect whether they enjoy playing with you, or if they start looking for the connection to end. Your body language can impact whether or not people will feel welcome walking up to you to ask you to play or spot. It can make the difference between skills feeling like fun or drudgery. Through experiences in jams and classes, you can learn a great deal about what your nonverbal communication may be expressing to others. The guidance we share here about your modes of communication will focus first on verbal communication, which can create a clear container for the rest of your contact. It can shift the ways other people connect with you in your Acro experiences and relationships.

One of the most powerful tools in any kind of verbal communication is the language that you choose to use. The concept of moving from "you need" statements to "I feel" or "we" statements is inspired by the work of Lux Sternstein,[2] one of the original teachers of AcroYoga in the United States. His focus on physical and emotional safety in the areas of spotting and conscious use of language has left a very positive impact on Acro communities around the world. Acro is fundamentally a relational practice that requires at least one partner to make something happen. That reality makes shared participation and mutual responsiveness central to the experience.

When sharing feedback or asking for changes during movements, using "you need" language refers to telling your partner what they are doing wrong, or what they need to change. This style of communication can create disconnection within a partnership by introducing blame and implying a position of superiority. When the dynamic is framed as though each person is separate from the shared situation, it can widen the distance between them, particularly when negative aspects are being emphasized. Even if one of the partners is more experienced than the other and trying to share their insight, this language can damage the connection.

Changing the style of language to "I feel" or "we" communication can be a powerful shift, and can cultivate a stronger and more trusting bond with the person you are engaging with. When asking for a change, or sharing your thoughts about the situation, use language that centers on your own perspective, such as "I feel," which expresses the sensations you are feeling in your own self or body. "I feel" statements keep the focus on yourself, and ideally, clearly bring your perspective to the interaction.

An extension of this language is "we" communication. Saying "let's focus on this technique together," instead of "you should focus on this technique," completely shifts the perspective. Redirecting the focus of your thought to an outcome that you and the other person want, and suggesting a way that both of you can take action to contribute to this outcome, creates space for each of you to lean into the shared reality. This language gives you an opportunity to share your experience and perspective, while offering solutions that both of you can work on together.

> *"A technique that now shows up in my romantic and Acro relationships is using 'we' to define the problem. We're in it together, and when both of us accept responsibility, we can grow together. It's not a silver bullet, but man, it goes a long way in setting a partnership up for success. During classes, jams, and festivals, I've always tried to team up with my partner against the challenge. It also helps to set expectations like, 'The world isn't going to end if we don't nail this skill today.' I'm a big believer in, 'If we succeed, let's go out for ice cream!' and also, 'If we fail, let's go out for ice cream!'" – A.J., Chicago Acro Community*

Inviting the other person into this kind of communication can be a matter of asking the simple question, "What do you need from me?" It is an act of care to shift away from telling the other person what you want, to asking how you can contribute to a better bond. It can open up a two-way dialogue that can cultivate a stronger connection. This type of language emphasizes collaboration over competition, or skills hierarchy.

Being open to others' feedback and requests can help you learn a great deal about yourself and about the impact you have on others. It is important to remember that the things you hear from others are mostly their perception of their world and their past experiences. This information should be used, but not taken as a judgment of your identity. It is important to remain aware of where your self is centered, where it ends, and where your interactions with the world outside you begins. You need to ensure that you take care of yourself as you are also caring for others. This is where the importance of boundaries comes in.

Understanding Boundaries and the Power of No

When you are interacting with other people or the world outside yourself, there are many boundaries you are naturally aware of and enforce for yourself. Some of these natural boundaries would be your skin, or your physical comfort zone. When someone to whom you haven't given consent touches you, you will likely move away from that touch; if someone stands too close, so they're inside your physical comfort zone, you may take a step back. For many people, navigating boundaries that are less innate may take more understanding and awareness. People doing Acro require that understanding and awareness. Creating healthy boundaries in a space where there is a high expectation of touch, takes intention and verbal communication, because there will be many different stances on personal boundaries. Being in these spaces with other people doing Acro regularly triggers different people's boundaries. Knowing beforehand how you would prefer to respond can alleviate many misunderstandings and provide a sense of control and personal agency.

Expanding on the deep-dive into boundaries in Chapter 7, there are many ways to navigate boundaries and cultivate more secure relationships. Knowing the foundations for communicating your own needs in relationships, and understanding the importance of boundaries, can be very helpful in keeping your relationships in a healthy place. A boundary is an expectation or limit you set for yourself in situations where you have control over your own response. Boundaries can take many different forms, including the standards you set for how you want to be treated by others. If constructive communication is one of your values for your relationships, then a boundary may be that you will not endure verbally abusive language. The significant thing to keep in mind about boundaries is that you yourself are responsible for enforcing your boundaries. In enforcing them, the consequences of those boundaries being crossed would be actions you take regardless of other people's involvement. If for instance, a boundary for yourself is to not listen to curse words, enforcing that boundary may look like leaving a room where someone is using profane language. Not storming out, just intentionally leaving.

Boundaries in Acro are important and healthy. This keeps everyone feeling safe. Your boundaries are a cue to others about how to treat you. As you set your own limits, it's important to remain aware of the boundaries others are trying to communicate to you as well. Building up the ability to firmly say “No” while playing with other people is a strong place to begin reinforcing your sense of your own boundaries. It can be a difficult step to know when to set a boundary in a situation where you are not certain of everything that may happen. As you feel more empowered to say “No” in these environments, you will be able to more enthusiastically say “Yes” to choices and experiences that you desire.

When you are clear with your boundaries, other people are able to respond appropriately to the standards of your interactions. When engaging with you, others will be able to trust your actions and responses. Others may not fully trust your “Yes” unless they trust your ‘No.”This trust in each other’s communication about boundaries is foundational to allowing you and your partner to commit to movements that may be dangerous or physically risky. This trust protects your nervous systems from triggering fight or flight responses. Acro is about synergy. That means that when you are able to trust the person you are playing with and the bond that you are creating, you will be able to master skills and movements that neither of you would be able to do on your own.

Loving relationships are synergistic as well. When you bond with and trust your partner, you will be able to accomplish much more together than you would be able to on your own. Both romantic and platonic love should always be mutual. Healthy love can only exist if both parties are willing to give and receive it. Establishing clear boundaries with a partner allows each person to truly see the other and embrace them entirely.

Develop an Openness to Connection

Once you have started to create a solid understanding of yourself and how you want to be treated, the next step is developing how you want to open yourself to connection. Having healthy relationships with the people around you will require a willingness to connect at various levels. This does not mean that you will need to be responsive to every bid for connection, but you should be aware when someone is trying to connect with you and how you would like to respond. Developing a state of openness within yourself and your relationships, can be cultivated through both intentional choices and practice within your relationships. One of the simplest ways to find this state of openness is by embracing your authentic self. Discovering how you want to bring your authentic self to your relational interactions can be done by understanding your values and setting standards for yourself and the world around you. Learn to cultivate a state of openness so that you can bring this to the people you want to be with.

To develop your state of openness, cultivate your sense of curiosity about people and the world outside of yourself. Nurture your sense of curiosity by adopting a beginner's mindset. Look for novel ways of doing things. You may need to try something uncommon, such as changing which hand you primarily do tasks with, or changing the path you take to get to work. Each of these experiments will open your mind to new inputs or points of view and expand on the questions you ask yourself. When you run into questions you don't know the answers to, be inquisitive and ask others for their perspectives or approaches. Each person thinks about things differently, so there are potential solutions and new questions in each person's response. Listen and observe their responses with an intention to understand, rather than trying to explain or share your own thoughts. With a sense of curiosity, it will be simple to open up to others as you try and find answers to the questions you have going through your mind.

In order to remain in a state of openness during difficult times, work to avoid getting overwhelmed and take action before getting in a heightened state of agitation. This means acknowledging your needs and limitations and asking for help. Give yourself grace and allow room for improvement. Treat yourself as you would treat a friend or loved one. You wouldn't expect them to be perfect, at least not every moment of every day, so you should change the expectations for yourself. Aim for excellence, not perfectionism. When you embrace the idea that everyone, including yourself, has qualities that may not please every other person, you can start to be kinder to yourself. You can start showing your authentic self to others without needing specific outcomes.

There will be times when you make mistakes and things don't bring the results you desire. Embrace those mistakes and experiences, for they give you an opportunity to learn and grow. Don't focus on not making mistakes at the expense of making attempts. As Stephen McCranie says, "The master has failed more times than the beginner has even tried."[3] One of the strongest ways to connect with your entire self is to use lessons learned from your past experiences, good and bad. A great time to ask for help is when you are feeling in over your head or at your limits.

One of the most important things to learn is that people actually want to help. Asking for help doesn't mean you are vulnerable or weak. Just the opposite. It is a powerful way to reinforce a state of presence and invite connection. As Simon Sinek has said, "We don't build trust by offering help, we build trust by asking for help."[4] Asking for help allows another person to connect and also share part of themselves in the interaction. When you ask for help before you become overwhelmed, you can engage a sense of curiosity about the situation. This can reinforce the relationship, especially when, after asking for help, you genuinely listen to the response and thank them even if you decide to go in a different direction. This isn't always the easiest thing for many people, especially depending on their history of relational experiences.

Recognizing defensiveness within yourself

While learning to become more open to feedback and the feelings of connection, it is common for a person to feel triggered by feedback and take it in the wrong way. This response is called defensiveness. In a defensive state, people often fall into old patterns that interfere with healthy, productive communication. A person being defensive can seek various ways of gaining a position of strength and superiority, such as relying on facts instead of feelings, asking for extremely clear communication from the other person, distracting from or evading the topic at hand, or even tearing down the other person's character to make them seem weaker. None of these tendencies contribute to building a strong relationship, let alone helping the other person feel heard or acknowledged. As Elizabeth Earnshaw, a marriage and family therapist working with the Gottman Institute, has shared,

> *When people are defensive, they are dismissive of the other person's point of view and their own responsibility in the matter, and they are unable to recognize that multiple realities exist. They struggle to see that listening and validating do not mean agreeing and that giving space to the other person does not mean you will never get space to share when the time is right.*[5]

It is important to become familiar with your own tendencies that signal you may be entering, or are already in a state of defensiveness. While there are many different tendencies that signal defensiveness, the most common show up as physiological symptoms in a person's body. This is in addition to a change in mental state. Examples of physical changes in the body can include a faster heart rate, more rapid breathing, and a tendency to hold the breath between sentences or between inhales and exhales. Some of the outwardly visible signs of this state may include using closed body language toward the person providing feedback, such as crossed arms, or agitated pacing while in conversation. This is a limited list, as these are only some of the signs that you may feel when you are getting into a defensive state. You will have to become aware of your own personal tendencies.

Noticing when your communication style changes while in a conversation or argument can be pivotal for turning a confrontation into a repairable moment. As Elizabeth Earnshaw writes, "There are very few scenarios in which we truly need to defend our point of view. Rather, we are mostly driven to do so by the desire to be right".[5] Some examples of changes in mental state or communication you may observe within yourself, or your partner, are responding before the other person has finished their sentence, over-explaining your reasoning or point of view, or using the word "but" frequently in responses.

When defensiveness begins to escalate during a confrontation, one person may begin interfering with what the other person is saying by not listening to their words, dismissing the other person's point of view, derailing the conversation, or even returning the blame to the other person, and potentially making themselves the victim. Pay attention to when you notice defensiveness in yourself and recognize your triggers. According to research by psychologists John Gottman and Nan Silver,[6] defensiveness is one of four communication habits dubbed The Four Horsemen, that are tied to an increased likelihood of separation or the end of a relationship.

There are many ways to help regulate your mood and reduce defensiveness when potentially triggering interactions arise. Reminding yourself of your values and firmest beliefs can help you feel less defensive and focused on what's truly important: pursuing your passions. If you are facing criticism that has triggered defensiveness, reframing the criticism as a sign of the other person's belief in you can help lower your defenses. When you know internally that your partner or someone close to you is only offering feedback because they have faith that you can accomplish great things, the criticism can take on a different tone. A more active way that you can defuse defensiveness is by using the "I feel" communication mentioned above. This approach also lessens the fuel for any confrontation, as no one can reasonably argue with or disprove your personal viewpoint or feelings.

Expectations vs Agreements vs Rules

This section will build on the communication methods laid out by describing the differences between expectations, agreements, and rules. A clear understanding of these differences can have a powerful impact on healthily navigating your relationships, within Acro or outside of it. When engaging with others to pull off a skill or movement, you may have an expectation of what you want to happen and how others are going to contribute to that outcome. However, without communicating with the other person how you intend to take action, you may unintentionally work against their contribution to the shared goal. Communicating how you and others will work together leads to synergy in the collaboration and allows for agreement with each other.

The agreements about how you will behave toward each other can create a space where you feel safe and confident that your actions will benefit the situation and the relationship. Sometimes situations arise where you must try to prevent certain actions, for instance keeping someone from touching or squeezing an injured body part. To keep certain actions from happening, you may put a rule on a situation or person, such as, "don't grab my wrist during this movement." These kinds of statements may or may not increase the collaboration within a relationship, but they are important for specific, and temporary, situations. It is also important to recognize when your communication becomes an expectation or rule, rather than an agreement. Digging in deeper on how each of these aspects work and how they can contribute to clearer communication, will give you more tools for improving your relationships.

Expectations

Expectations are views that you have of yourself, or other people, on how you believe things to be. Expectations can be implicitly understood or explicitly communicated. Expressing an expectation does not mean that the other person is bound to behave according to your idea of what should happen. Understanding your own expectations can be helpful, because they often reveal the beliefs you hold about a person or situation. Knowing the expectations others have for you can help you interact with them in ways that can be pleasing for everyone. For instance, knowing the expectations for a job can help you navigate the behaviors you need to take in order to be successful and feel that you have a fulfilling relationship with your supervisor or clients.

When engaging in Acro, sharing your expectations for what kinds of skills you want to try, or are open to, helps the other people decide whether they want to try the same kinds of skills, or if they feel confident to keep you safe while trying them. Having those expectations without sharing them can create situations where you don't get to try the things you want. Others may not be prepared for the movements you have in mind before attempting them, which can potentially lead to injuries. Even if each person has expressed different expectations, there can be room for collaboration. When each expectation is allowed recognition, the potential is there for a compromise or mutually beneficial option. It is important to know and understand your own expectations. It can be even more impactful, to share them with others when appropriate.

> *"More than once, a Flyer has said things like, 'You're my Base now,' or interrupted my play with others to assert ownership or control. Those partnerships didn't last, but the wild part is that I've caught myself doing something similar. I'll start working with a flyer, things go really well, and then I begin acting as if my own needs, desires, and goals should come first at jams or classes. Of course that isn't true, but I think a lot of us can relate to that impulse. Now, as part of my practice, I try to give everyone as much space as possible and make myself available when acrobats want to work on something. As my practice has evolved, building a strong, inclusive community has become more important than learning new skills." – A.J., Chicago Acro Community*

Agreements

One extension of expressed expectations leads into the realm of agreements. Conversations about establishing agreements should not start by expressing each person's expectations. Instead, express your desired outcomes. Once your desires for how you both see the situation, or your relationship, have been expressed, you can find common ground that you both are invested in. Then an agreement can be established. In creating agreements, the desires of both parties should be expressed and included. Ideally both parties will communicate and work together to set out expectations for how their desires can be fulfilled through the agreement. For instance, when deciding to train more frequently with an Acro partner, setting an agreement on how often you will train together may start with sharing desires for how often each week you both want, and then working through the details of your schedules. Coming to an agreement that both of you can realistically fulfill sets the stage for each person showing up for the relationship.

There may be relationships in your life that rely on implicit, unspoken agreements, such as family systems where conflict is not revisited after it has ended. The uncertainty caused by unclear agreements can introduce hesitance into a relationship. Part of you is working diligently toward the desired result, while another is subconsciously aware that not everyone is on the same page. With clearly communicated and consenting agreements, relationships become more adept at resolving situations through a strengthened bond and transparency. The goal of agreements is to give everyone involved a clear understanding of how to treat each other, especially in ways that are appreciated. They allow each person to fully bring themselves into interactions.

Rules

Rules are restrictions that one person imposes on another person, with or without their consent. The intention with rules is typically to control or enforce certain kinds of behaviors on other people, not necessarily for their benefit. While rules may be helpful in impersonal scenarios where there is limited information or understanding, rules may not be helpful in relationships where the people setting the rules are well acquainted with the people affected. An instance where rules are imposed on others impersonally would be a locked-door rule that a fitness studio imposes on clients who are 15 minutes late. The studio doesn't know why you may be late, or if it would truly be disruptive to the class to let you in, but they set those rules for your behavior regardless. Those kinds of rules are impersonal and apply to any person in the group. Rules in many interpersonal situations leave the person who is affected by the rule feeling restricted, unsafe, and untrusted.

There is a significant difference in how we describe rules versus agreements in the context of secure relationships. If rules are used between two people, it's better that they be used only on a temporary basis, with an end date in mind. In cases like this, they may come to be more like agreements than rules. We consider agreements to have a collaborative nature, where each affected person is involved in creating the essence of the agreement. With rules, there is typically one or more "ruling person" who creates constraints that other people have to follow, or deal with the consequences. The premise of one partner not cooking certain foods in the kitchen can be an agreement if everyone in the house decides on it together in solidarity. But would it be an agreement if one person who's allergic set the expectation for everyone else? No. It has become a rule. The difference in intention affects how other people respond and feel about restrictions, which is an important consideration to make when embracing healthier communication and relationships.

When each of us becomes more aware of these concepts, it allows our relationships and interactions to nurture expression and curiosity for each of us. When we are able to be curious about others and the world around us, we are able to explore and share our experiences with the people who are important to us. Sharing more of who we are in our relationships strengthens our bonds and invites others to bring more of themselves into the relationship. Relationships in which you feel safe and secure are the ones that you want to contribute to more and not abandon. The same goes for others.

Creating the relationships that you want in your life starts with understanding how you are showing up in your interactions. By understanding yourself and your needs, and communicating these to the people around you, you can create clearer understanding and expectations that allow others to step into their confidence in interactions with you. The confidence that they can behave in ways that feel comfortable for them, and that they can contribute without being penalized or blamed, allows for more feelings of enjoyment and love toward you. When you build a relationship within this space of clear communication, commitment, and awareness, you will be able to nurture a healthy, secure, attachment-based relationship.

Notes

1. *Tea and Consent, video, produced by Blue Seat Studios for Thames Valley Police and the Thames Valley Sexual Violence Prevention Group, 2015, YouTube.*
2. *"Trust + Communication (w/ Lux Sternstein)," episode of Sorry to Podcast This, November 13, 2019.*
3. *Stephen McCranie, "Be Friends with Failure," in Brick by Brick, StephenMcCranie.com.*
4. *Simon Sinek, "Asking for Help Is an Act of Service."*
5. *Elizabeth Earnshaw, "Can You Defend Yourself Without Being Defensive? Here's How to Respond to Criticism the Right Way," mindbodygreen, November 27, 2019.*
6. *Gottman and Silver, The Seven Principles for Making Marriage Work.*

9

Broad Strokes of Being AcroSecure

When you begin to notice the connections that naturally arise in each Acro movement, you start to see how your body and movements have a direct impact on your partner. It's easy to get caught up in focusing only on your part: how to balance, how to stay strong, how to improve your personal technique. But without taking into account your partner's experience, their needs, their ability to execute, and how your movements might affect them, you might find yourself making things difficult for both of you. The magic really happens when you begin to sense how your choices, timing, and adjustments directly influence your partner's experience. If you stay locked in your own sensations, trying to muscle through or perfect your portion in isolation, you can unintentionally make things harder. But when you slow down just enough to notice where your partner is, what they need, or how you can make space for their effort to land more fully, the whole dynamic becomes smoother and more collaborative.

Sometimes, it's something as simple as softening your tone,

matching their timing, or shifting your focus to support their stability. These subtle shifts communicate care, trust, and presence, qualities that are just as important in Acro as they are in any meaningful relationship. In so doing, you're not just creating stronger skills, you're building the kinds of dynamics that feel safer, more reciprocal, and more fulfilling. And while having a good sense of what makes for a strong, resilient partnership is a great start, it's the actions you take: how you show up, how you respond, and how you adjust that truly strengthen the bonds between you. When you're able to bring this level of care and consideration to your partnerships, it invites them to do the same. This creates a shared space where trust and possibility can grow.

As you understand how you fit into healthy and fulfilling relationships, it is also important to understand how you can consider the other person in your relationship. When you are able to understand your needs and desires from the relationship, you can better communicate and act in ways that have intention. The people in your life will respond to your intentions, and they can be more certain about how you may fit into their lives. When there is both agreement and comfort in how you fit into each other's lives and support networks, trust is nurtured and more ease is found within interactions.

The methods in this chapter significantly improve the relationships you can have with all the meaningful people in your life, but not all relationships with the people in your life will need to have clear intentions. Even when interactions are less structured in nature, or just casual, they can also be fulfilling. There are many ways that you can nurture your relationships with others, whether you want an attachment-based relationship or not.

Intentions can be conveyed through verbal communication of your expectations, boundaries, or desires. Directly approaching your relationships with a sense of intention may be jarring in the beginning, depending on how you have related to others in the past. The sense that you may be changing or disrupting an existing relationship dynamic can trigger fear or even grief. The positive aspect is that communicating your new intentions often results in the other person responding to the change quickly and the two of you finding a new rapport and a new dynamic. The intentionality that you bring into a relationship helps the other person enter the interaction with more clarity. They're more able to consent and match your intention with their own intentions and enthusiasm. Bringing this to your Acro dynamics can make the difference between asking someone to play, starting from l-basing bird to calibrate, versus asking someone to try a specific skill and finding relevant progressions to calibrate. While both instances may allow enjoyable experiences that build rapport and learning, the latter will allow both people to know a desired trajectory and move toward that goal more efficiently.

Taking a bit of time to understand your intention, or the other person's intention for an interaction can open up numerous pathways to healthily navigate and support each other. On top of that, you might know what tools can help improve the interaction. Some of these you can learn from this book. You will learn others from the supporting materials at the end of this book, or from your past experiences. Having repeated positive interactions within your relationships encourages others to trust and reach out to you more often. They may ask you to help them feel connected and comforted, or feel centered during risky ventures. When you are there for them in ways that they appreciate and can receive, they will feel cared for. This is an essential part of nurturing your relationships and creating an Acro dynamic that allows both of you to grow, learn, and thrive.

Ways to Be There For Your Partner

To respond well to your partner, there are several tools and practices worth developing so they are available to you when situations arise. While you may be approaching your relationships with more clarity and intention, the people you are interacting with may not be as intentional, or have had the opportunity to read this book. Just because they are not approaching relationships in the same way you are does not mean that the relationship won't be healthy or meaningful. Each person will bring a unique contribution to a relationship with you. The relationship dynamic between the two of you will be the result of both of your contributions. You have the power to significantly impact the resulting relationship dynamic, with or without their informed buy-in. To bring a relationship closer to a more fulfilling dynamic, you may have to set the example first. This may be by initiating a discussion about intentions, or by acting in alignment to how you would like both of you to enter into each interaction. You may set the example by asking for consent more often, or showing curiosity about their emotional life outside of the

Acro environment.

When you desire for both of you to be more open, honest, considerate, or intimate, you may need to shift your focus to how you can be more supportive, enjoyable, honest, or desirable from the perspective of the other person. You will have to surpass the "Golden Rule," and embrace the "Platinum Rule": "Do unto others as *they* would want to be done to them." You cannot only treat others as you want to be treated in relationships. You have to take the initiative to listen and understand how they want to be treated in each interaction. When they feel that interactions with you are positive experiences for them, they will desire to have more interactions with you and will be more open and committed to respect the boundaries and agreements that you have set. Your consideration of their experience will encourage them to be considerate of yours as well. To further your journey of helping the people in your life feel more positive, we want to give a primer into frameworks such as love languages, active listening, and attachment roles.

> *"The best advice I've been given is to ask for what I want, not what I don't want, and to frame it around what I want my partner to feel rather than what I want to feel. And sometimes you just don't know. In those moments, the best thing you can do is take a breath, think about what's happening, and talk it out together. The most important thing is to bring positive energy, because whether you're angry or sad, that transfers just as much as excitement, fun, relaxation, or care. Breathing and communicating with*

awareness of both my emotions and my partner's can help create more positive experiences." – C.S., Texas AcroYoga Community

Not everyone will appreciate the same gestures of appreciation in the same way. Telling someone they did a great job during the skill may cause someone to smile broadly, while another person may prefer a high five to spark the same level of happiness. While both gestures are generally understood as positive acknowledgement, the effectiveness of each gesture is different depending on the person. There are multiple ways to convey appreciation or affection; understanding which way each person is most receptive can greatly improve the positive impact of your actions. The work by Gary Chapman on love languages groups the gestures into five categories: words of affirmation, acts of service, quality time, physical touch, and gift giving.[1] According to Chapman, certain types of gestures resonate more strongly with an individual depending on their preferred language of affection. Gestures from a less impactful category are not necessarily harmful, but when most expressions of care do not align with what feels most meaningful to a person, they can begin to feel underappreciated in the relationship. Understanding when to celebrate and show appreciation through certain gestures can take your relationships from enjoyable to highly enthusiastic.

On the flip side, you can use the concepts of love languages to understand better ways to give feedback or criticism. Different people will react to messages of criticism differently depending on the method of delivery. In addition, while most people would welcome appreciation at any time, successfully giving feedback or criticism is sensitive to the timing of the delivery. One person may be open and want verbal feedback directly after the instance, while another person may be more fragile and vulnerable with that timing and prefer to wait until later to be told in a written message.

You should also be aware that some people may be sensitive to time and absences. They may read into a lessening of the amount or frequency of time spent together as a criticism connected somehow to the events preceding the change. Having clear and understood communication about sharing negative feelings within your relationships can smooth out many assumptions that are made in the absence of a secure relationship.

When there are doubts about how a person may appreciate feedback or criticism, it is a good practice to ask them beforehand if they are open to receiving feedback at this time. For situations where there are questions in your mind about whether the other person will receive your message in a positive impression, it can be appropriate to ask them if you can share. Then stay open to listen and respect their answer.

Listening to Connect and Support

The act of listening is more nuanced and powerful than most people give it credit for. The neurological processes that activate when you hear a sentence vary depending on your prior state of mind. Besides the significant difference between being distracted or defensive, versus actively listening, there are different states of mind within active listening.[2] The ways that you listen can be a powerful method for helping the people in your life feel positive emotions, and leave your interactions feeling better than they did at the start. We will focus on three of these states, the ones that we find most useful for nurturing non-professional relationships: listening to support, listening to connect, and listening to solve.

The first method of listening that is significantly helpful is listening to support. In this mode, the intention is to hear what the other person is sharing and to acknowledge that you hear them without imposing your own viewpoint in your response. This can include finding ways to give positive encouragement or sympathy for their perspective. Understanding when to engage in this mode can greatly improve and sustain your rapport with the other person.

It is fairly common for people to misjudge how to respond in these interactions. They often offer advice or try to fix the expressed situation. When this happens, it is easy for the person sharing to feel unheard, judged, or even belittled. This is not what either person intends, but without clear expectations, there is a larger chance of misunderstanding of intention or interpretation. A signal that can help identify when this method of listening is called for is if the person sharing is not speaking about you, someone you directly know, or an issue you are directly responsible for. When you pick up on this signal, resort to the mode of listening to support until the person sharing asks for further opinions or advice.

Listening to connect is done with the intention of hearing how the sharer would like to interact with you. This type of listening can vary greatly, from simply hearing someone's experiences because they want to share with you, to engaging in a deeper conversation where both people are genuinely curious to hear and understand each other's perspectives. Some examples are, someone telling you about their day because they care and want to share with you, or sharing their thoughts about the class you took together and wanting to hear your thoughts about the class also. There is space to empathize with the other person while connecting this way.

When listening in this state of mind, continue to be curious about what the other person is saying. They will have a reason why they are engaging with you. Even though there may be a call for your input, ensure that you are relating to what the other person is talking about, and not getting preoccupied with your own response or perspective. At times, a person may be sharing only to update you, without wanting to go deeper into the topic. In those moments, respecting their cues and allowing the conversation to move elsewhere can be an expression of care. Honoring their intentions communicates care and helps strengthen the trust they are offering you.

This third method of listening is listening to solve. This state of mind comes more naturally to many people and is often the default when talking to others. The thought that something can be fixed or improved can cause a person to focus solely on the content of a problem. When you focus on the problem alone, and not on the person speaking about it, there may be a disconnection with the full scope of the problem, and the person. As you adopt this state of listening, be sure to continue listening to the whole message and engage with the other person as you discuss possible solutions.

Rarely will someone come to you asking for the entire answer. This method of listening should not be the one used most often within the relationships you are trying to nurture. This method of listening can be particularly helpful when used before or after a problem occurs, separate from when it's an immediate issue.

During Acro play, the communication that others are sharing will require multiple methods of listening and frequent switching between methods. Your listening flexibility will be essential to connecting and building rapport with others when first meeting up. They may be sharing how they are feeling in their body or mind, sharing about what happened before they arrived, or maybe setting intentions about what they are comfortable doing during the session. Your ability to listen openly and respond in ways that match the others' intention will contribute to the connection and enjoyment of the interaction for all of you.

When a person talks about how to improve a skill attempt with you, there will be more context in what they are saying than just the physical mechanics. They will potentially be sharing how the attempt felt to them, and if it was comfortable or overwhelming. If they are expressing a sense of overwhelm, there may be things that you can "fix" in the movement, but you may also need to use one of the other listening methods to help them feel more supported and connected.

Knowing when to use each method of listening will take understanding either the needs or intention of the person talking to you. Ask them what kind of response or feedback they would appreciate at that moment. You can make the invitation simple by having signals or codewords with your partner to share when there is any question about how to engage. This is really helpful when asking for, or giving verbal feedback during or after attempting a skill. Knowing whether or not your partner needs encouragement to feel better about trying again, or needs more information to help them build awareness within the skill, will improve their ability to make adjustments and feel comfortable doing so.

Roles You Can Serve in Your Relationships

One of the contemporary ideas of what it means to be an attachment-based partner in many frameworks, is that an attachment partner serves as both a safe haven and a secure base.[3] To feel securely-attached in our relationships, we need to feel we have **safe havens** to turn to whenever and for whatever reason. We also need to know that when a safe space is established, we can turn away from it and engage with the world while maintaining connection to it.

This space can be a purely emotional safe space. A **secure base** serves as the platform from which we move out into the world. In simplified terms, being a safe haven serves the role of accepting and being with someone as they are. A secure base serves the role of supporting them in growing beyond who they are.

In our modern world, where we are expected to meet the needs of so many roles and expectations, it can be difficult to consistently fill both of these roles in every attachment-based relationship that we are part of. It can be challenging for a romantic partner to always meet the needs of being a safe haven and secure base, especially as those needs for each role may continuously change as your situation changes. When you lean into multiple attachment-based relationships, you may want to rely on different people at different times. This depends on what they have available to give and your comfort level with them. Understand with compassion that you can choose who you turn to, and that others can choose to turn back toward you. These times of choice can create a broader sense of support so that when one person may not be able to be your safe haven or secure base at a particular time, you won't have to feel abandoned.

In our search for relationship safety, our attachment system is always on the lookout for answers to some core concerns.[4] It wants to know that if we turn to our partner, they will be there for us and accept us as we are without judgment or criticism. We need to feel that they will comfort us and respond in ways that soothe our nervous system. Underneath it all is the fundamental need to know that we matter, that we make a difference in these moments, and that we can lean into and rely on each other when times get tough. These are the quiet questions at the heart of secure connections. Being mindful of them can help us navigate our relationships with more care and intention.

Having people in our training spaces who can serve in these roles create a more supportive and comfortable training environment in which to explore. While teachers can focus on ensuring safety, they also may encourage exploration and advancement. These roles can also be fulfilled by other people in your training space or community. We will cover the ways that you and your partner can establish safe havens or secure base roles. We will also consider whether or not the relationship you have with each person serves more of one role than the other. In addition, you can serve as a safe haven or secure base for yourself at times. What might that look like?

Being a Safe Haven for Each Other

One of the essential roles that you can serve in a healthy attachment-based relationship is being there for your partner when they reach out to connect, or they turn toward you for reassurance. Acting as a safe haven for someone during stressful times can help them feel less anxious in general, and also more secure in your presence. It will bolster your relationship with them. When your partner feels that you accept them as they are, are concerned for their safety, and can respond to their distress, it helps them regulate their nervous system. It is a source of emotional and physical support and comfort.

When you have people in your life who serve as safe-haven relationships, research shows that you may be more resilient in the face of high levels of stress and traumatic events. When people have their safe-haven attachment figures around them, either during or soon after a stressful event, they recover faster, experience less long-term physical and emotional pain, and are less likely to have escalating symptoms of PTSD.[5] The presence of someone like this during Acro can deepen a person's sense of safety when approaching skills or forms of play that feel outside their comfort zone. When one or more people in the space, including their Spotter, help create that sense of safety, participants are often more willing to try new skills and are better able to grow quickly. A common saying in the wider Acro community is "each Acro community grows only as skilled as their most skilled Spotters"

The actions that you can do to be a safe haven for the people in your life begin with offering acceptance. Accept all aspects of the other person unconditionally, including the positives, negatives, things you agree with, and things you disagree with. Showing them unconditional acceptance reinforces their esteem. It lets them know they're lovable, interesting, valuable, and cared for. For you to be seen as a safe haven, they need to feel that you accept them for who they are and do not want to change them or their identity. Acceptance, in this context, means helping people feel that they do not have to hide, perform, or change who they are in order to be received with care. In practice, it looks like listening with openness, validating what they feel, respecting their dignity, and helping them feel that all of who they are can be met with care. This kind of acceptance creates the foundation for attunement, because it allows you to notice and respond to the other person as they actually are, rather than as you assume them or want them to be.

Additional actions that you can do in this role are to give emotional support and comfort. When you are interacting with them, ask how they feel and listen to them with your full attention. Share reassurance when they are unsure. One way to show support is to validate a loved one's feelings when they talk about an emotional experience. For example, "Wow, that sounds really frightening," or

"Yeah, I would have been surprised too." Inquire about their day, ask about things that happened, or talk about things that are important to each of you. When they are in need, such as when they're sick, tired, or overwhelmed, find practical ways to help support them get through their day or week. When people know they can rely on you when things get tough, they will feel fortified that they are not going through life alone. They will know who to turn to when things get tough.

> *"My new body worker has done this for me during my last few sessions. She really set the scene and expressed that there was no emotion or expression that would be too much and that all of me was welcome. It really helped me feel safe as some uncomfortable emotions did come up and I felt safe to release them and express them without fearing judgement." –N.B., Texas AcroYoga Community*

To be another person's safe haven, you should show that you are responsive to when they may be in need. Track what is going on in each other's lives and make sure to follow up and inquire about those events. Responsiveness in adult relationships involves conveying understanding, care, and warmth. The purpose of responsiveness is to make the other person feel valued, that they have your attention, they are understood, and that they're comfortable in your presence. Being responsive does not mean you need to be physically available when it is impossible for you to be so. It means you are emotionally available, regardless of whether or not you want to be. It also means you communicate when you do not have the capacity to be available, before they are in drastic need.

Being a Secure Base for Each Other

Once a person feels safe within themselves or in their relationships, they have more freedom to turn outward and engage with the wider world. When someone knows they have people they can count on, it provides a secure foundation from which to explore, take risks, and try new things. Acting as a secure base for someone means offering support and encouragement that allows them to grow and fully express who they are. At times, this requires risk taking. At other times, it means taking a break from each other. This support can take many forms depending on each person. It can be in the form of offering guidance when solicited, calling us out in empathetic ways, or functioning as a compassionate mirror for our blind spots. While being a person's secure base may potentially sound like fun, it also takes effort and time to establish the security required so the person can feel safe to indulge their curiosity in activities outside of the relationship and then safely return to the relationship with our acceptance.

Having an attachment figure serves as a base of security that allows a person to explore their environment with confidence. In support of this role, you should be able to reliably welcome them on their return, comfort them if they are upset, and reassure them if they are overwhelmed. A secure-base partner is available to help remove obstacles when their person encounters a problem too much to handle. When they are in distress, and when they are in need, a secure base is non-interfering. You support exploration by not controlling or interfering unnecessarily. Secure-base partners encourage and accept exploration, thereby motivating each other to take on challenges, pursue personal goals, and grow through learning and discovery.

One of the first things you can do to be a secure base for another person is to encourage their personal growth and development. Inquire and listen to their dreams, ideas, and visions. Support each other's work or interests. Encouraging growth is about showing your openness to their thoughts about the world. Showing interest could also involve asking questions like, "How has work been?" or "How is everything going?" If they open up about a difficult experience, try your best not to judge, criticize, or jump to conclusions. Instead, be curious and ask questions for clarification. Secure-base actions in Acro include encouraging exploration without pressure, offering guidance without taking over, cooperating instead of controlling, respecting boundaries, and helping a partner regulate challenge by suggesting progressions, offering a spot, scaling a skill to match their readiness, and creating an environment that feels manageable enough for them to try again with confidence. Acknowledge their capabilities and possibilities for growth. Help them make an impact on their world.

> *"My new partner is into Acro. He's been doing it for years, and he introduced me to it. I felt it was important to try it so I could better understand something he's so excited about. I have sports performance anxiety, and he knows I've been struggling to go to big jams with him. He suggested I take*

some lessons and meet other beginners so I could build friendships and maybe find a beginner crew to go with to bigger jams. That way, instead of feeling intimidated and anxious about being alone and no one wanting to work with me, I'd have my own support group. He also came to a smaller, more beginner-friendly jam with me and reassured me he would only play with me and stay by my side so my anxiety would be easier to manage. He even politely refused working with someone else, saying he was spending time with me that day. That meant the world to me while I sat there awkwardly on the mat, heart racing, fiddling with my jewelry, waiting for him to come back." –A.L., Canadian Acro Community

As you support their exploration, be sure to display sensitivity and a genuine willingness to help the other person. Make this evident through your behavior, tone of voice, and words. Be emotionally available to connect when interacting and offer words of encouragement when they take on new responsibilities, take a risk, or learn something new. This could mean celebrating the courage it takes for them to step into unfamiliar territory. Acknowledge the effort they're putting in by simply saying, "I see how hard you're working, and I'm proud of you." At times, you may also need to compassionately bring light to your partner's limitations and blind spots, so that they may readjust and continue their journey as they see fit. For example, you might gently point out when they're holding back out of fear, or when a certain pattern is getting in the way of their growth. In these moments, aim to speak with kindness and empathy, so they feel supported rather than criticized. This balanced approach, offering both encouragement and constructive feedback, nurtures an environment where they can feel safe enough to stretch beyond their comfort zone, while still knowing that you'll be there to support them no matter what.

Another action that supports being a secure base is being cooperative. Cooperation looks like working with the other person to resolve issues, instead of stepping in and solving the issue for them. Cooperation in adult relationships is about allowing the other person to have agency in the process, without trying to change, control, or direct them in specific ways. Oftentimes in Acro dynamics where one person is more skilled or experienced than the other, it can be simple for the more experienced person to make the skill work, either by forcing the other person to move in a certain way or guiding them through the entire movement. This direct level of involvement in achieving success can interfere with the less experienced person's ability to explore and figure out a solution on their own. This behavior is in opposition to the principle of being cooperative. Staying cooperative can be challenging, especially if you don't agree with the other person's thoughts or behaviors. But when you are able to stay within cooperation principles and support the other person's exploration and understanding, when they do find success, they can be more appreciative of the support given during the process.

One of the other important actions that is key to being a secure base is encouraging equality in resolutions and the relationship. One way to foster equality is both offering and seeking knowledgeable input and emotional support. You could do this by asking for their opinion on something you need help with and offering them support in return. There are many times in Acro where two people working together have a significant difference in experience, their standing in the community, or situational authority. The best way to balance out a power dynamic is to be open and honest. Respect the other person's boundaries and support their individuality and interests. Have conversations about things that are intellectually or emotionally stimulating to each other. Another fundamental component of achieving equality with the other person is to show that you trust them and their perspective.

As you engage in more fulfilling relationships and interactions, you will be able to both understand your own needs and intentions and consider your partner. You will be able to better relate to their experience. This will create a healthy relationship dynamic. There will be many directions that you can take the relationship as you both understand the capabilities of the other and what you each have to offer. Whether you want to be there for your partner as an attachment figure, just in the role of a safe haven or secure base, or enjoying a temporary fulfilling experience with each other, the ability to provide positive feelings to another person through your interactions will create opportunities for your relationships to grow and develop in healthy directions. Learning how to nurture not only yourself and another person, but also the relationship itself will create a sustainable culture that enhances the environment for both of you to grow toward each other.

Notes

1. *Gary D. Chapman, The Five Love Languages: How to Express Heartfelt Commitment to Your Mate (Chicago: Northfield, 1995).*
2. *Jeff Joireman, Tiffany L. Needham, and April L. Cummings, "Relationships between Dimensions of Attachment and Empathy," North American Journal of Psychology 4, no. 3 (2002): 63–80.*
3. *Ainsworth, "Attachments and Other Affectional Bonds across the Life Cycle," 35.*
4. *Bowlby, Separation, 202, 359.*
5. *Patricia Frazier, Kelly Greer, Leslie A. Gabrielsen, Courtney Tennen, Annette M. Park, and Tomich, "The Roles of Social Support in Recovery from Stress and Trauma," in The Oxford Handbook of Stress and Mental Health, ed. Kate Harkness and Elizabeth P. Hayden (New York: Oxford University Press, 2020).*

10

The ACRO of Being AcroSecure

Diving into a relationship with a romantic partner, Acro partner, or even friends, can be an intensely fulfilling experience. The curiosity that builds as layers are unraveled, and the comfort available as we build familiarity, can truly be one of the treasures of life. They are woven from moments of shared laughter, silent understanding, and the small gestures that make each of us feel safe and seen. Healthy relationships hold space for our vulnerabilities and the parts of ourselves that are still in the process of growing. These relationships can be places where we learn about ourselves, experience joy, and practice being both fully present and deeply engaged.

The art of creating and maintaining these connections goes beyond just sharing good times. It involves a steady, intentional effort to nurture the partnership as it evolves. It's about showing up when things feel easy, and when they feel challenging, about bringing genuine curiosity to our partner's experience and sharing our own. It's in these moments that we discover the rich potential of a secure and resilient partnership, one that can truly sustain and uplift us both over time. While scientific frameworks can offer valuable tools for understanding and supporting the art of building relationships, every relationship is ultimately unique. The individuals involved bring their own experiences, personalities, and circumstances, creating something new each time.

While a neurochemical cocktail can intensify the early feelings of attraction, excitement, emotional closeness, and reward, a relationship's fulfillment does not need to decline once that initial rush begins to calm. Longevity can be enhanced and leaned into by developing a healthy relationship dynamic that supports both of you. Building a secure attachment relationship can provide the feelings that can keep you both coming back to each other and allow both of you to find even more enjoyment from the other parts of your lives. Restating from earlier chapters, secure attachment relationships do not have to be with a romantic partner, but many dedicated Acro-partner dynamics do become attachment-based relationships. The principles in this book and chapter are all about helping you grow all your attachment-based relationships into secure and solid connections.

It's helpful to think of your relationship as its own separate entity, something you both create and shape together. Even if you and your partner are individually thriving, the relationship still needs care and attention to grow and flourish. Just as you invest in each other, it's important to also invest in the relationship itself. The relationship has its own needs. It takes on qualities from both of you, shaped by your agreements, shared experiences, and how you've treated one another over time. When both partners consistently contribute time, care, and affection, not just to each other but to the relationship, you create a foundation that can support you both, especially during moments when one of you may be feeling low or out of sync. A strong, well-nourished partnership can offer a sense of stability, joy, and resilience. Additionally, it can provide energy and comfort through both easeful and more challenging times.

Getting into the specifics of being AcroSecure, we have broken it out into four principles with the acronym "ACRO." Embracing each of these principles into your partnership, and other relationships, will enhance the connection between the two of you. These four principles can be implemented in your daily practice, either all at once or by focusing on each one individually for each practice session. In our experience with coaching and working alongside many partnerships throughout our Acro history, these following four areas are some of the most important takeaways. We believe they are core to successful partnerships. They are the recurring aspects of Acro that have helped improve our relationships when implemented.

The A in ACRO: Attunement to Build Trust

In the practice of Acro, having a strong attunement can really enhance the quality of movement with each partner. Attunement is tuning into the subtle signals and rhythms of another person, whether in Acro, conversation, or daily life. It's about really noticing how another person is feeling, where they're at, and what they might need in the moment. In practice, it can be as simple as matching the level of energy they're bringing, responding with a gentle tone when they're feeling tender, or adjusting your movements in Acro to sync with their balance and pace. Partnerships that are attuned to each other notice how each body is moving on a particular day to respond to each other efficiently and create a synergy in movement. When you're doing a skill with someone you're really attuned to, it often takes less energy and effort. Your body naturally reduces tension because it trusts the connection. In contrast, when doing that same skill with another experienced partner who you're less familiar with can feel more effortful, as your nervous system stays on alert. It may recruit extra muscle to brace for unexpected movements.

Having a partnership that promotes rapid growth and enjoyment of a physical practice like Acro requires a pretty high level of trust to support your comfort while trying new things. Expanding your own comfort zone while being close to another person takes a connection that feels safe. Unthreatening. After finding that you want a close partnership, there are ways to build a space, and relationship, for that to flourish.

One aspect of getting comfortable with each other is attuning to your partner's presence and perspective. This does not mean that you have to agree with them and accept their experience as your own, but that you are willing to join them in their inner state of mind and inner physical experience. It means you empathize with what they are going through. Building a partnership that feels strongly attuned is essential for creating a secure bond and relationship. When you're in sync and truly tuned in to each other's needs and rhythms, you create a foundation of trust and understanding that helps both of you feel safe and supported.

On a physical level, your body attunes to people that are consistently within your personal presence. This physical process can be consciously sped up by extended touch or breathing in sync with each other. The ways that we attune to different partners may also be very different. On a cognitive level, your mind attunes by learning enough about the other person so that you can reasonably predict how they will respond to different situations. You can help this mental process along by staying curious and asking questions that feel natural or resonate with your personal values. On an emotional level, you start to feel more at ease when you see how your partner handles intense emotions, whether it's excitement, frustration, or stress. Practicing and learning new skills together can help this emotional attunement happen faster.

As you practice attuning to someone else, you might start to notice subtle sensations and thoughts arising that seem to center around them. It's that feeling of being truly seen, understood, and felt by another person. That's what it feels like to be connected in a way that goes beyond words. You may notice and become aware quickly when your partner is having an "off-day," when something may be bothering them. They may have a small injury that they haven't told you about yet, but you feel something is off about your movements together. They may have had a stressful day or week that is making them more tense. They may not be as expressive as normal. Having this awareness can be helpful in knowing whether to inquire if something is bothering them, or give them space to share. Oftentimes, the act of sharing, or even inquiring, can bring the partnership back into sync, so that a practice session can be productive and enjoyable without the unspoken disconnection.

Over time, when there is enough attunement between you and your partner, you may also become attuned to the relationship itself. You may start to feel supported and seen, simply by knowing that you're in a relationship that you both value. This attunement can deepen the trust and security you feel with each other. You might also start to notice, either consciously or intuitively, when something in the relationship dynamic shifts. These shifts are natural and can be important signals that it's time to pause and have a conversation. Sharing your concerns or feelings can help you both stay connected and, if needed, adjust the expectations or agreements you have together. Keeping communication open in this way helps nurture a healthy and evolving relationship.

Even in attuned, attachment-based partnerships, difficulties will surface. Partners may need to learn how to remain attuned when one person is upset, how to stay connected when old triggers are activated, and how to navigate moments when jealousy arises. These challenges do not mean the relationship is failing. Rather, they are part of the ongoing work of learning how to return to one another with greater care, clarity, and connection. We will speak more about each of these challenges in a later chapter on maintaining established attachment-based relationships.

The C in ACRO: Celebrate Astonishment

There are so many ups and downs within the practice of Acro. Learning new skills with another person is exhilarating and hard. Having these ups and downs repeatedly with a partner creates an environment that lends effectively to the establishment of an attachment-based bond. Celebrating moments of joy and delight with a partner creates many reinforcing emotions for each of you. Honoring these moments can be expressed through words of affirmation, actions, touch, and even the way you look at each other.

One of the foundational elements of secure attachment is expressed delight, as noted by Daniel P. Brown and David Elliott.[1] Expressed delight is also required for promoting a healthy sense of self within a secure relationship. When partners celebrate not only moments of joy, but also each person who played a part in creating them, it deepens appreciation and reinforces a sense of being valued and special within the relationship. Having this practice of gratitude, and articulating the ways that each partner values the other, creates a culture of positivity in the partnership that allows for mutual vulnerability, authenticity, and the desire to grow.

Incorporating this practice of celebrating delight is essential to establishing a partnership and practice that can grow for multiple months and years. When practicing in a partnership, you can only be fueled by the enthusiasm of an external teacher, coach, or group for so long. At the beginning of your practice together, it can be really helpful and enjoyable to practice in a jam or class setting with some frequency. This creates moments to find excitement in new material you are learning together, and lets you find a shared norm in style.

As your partnership develops and your practice becomes more uniquely your own, you will likely spend more time centered on each other and your shared movement. When the majority of time together is focused within your partnership, it's important to generate the enthusiasm of spending time together by sparks from each of you. Embrace the delight that you get to acknowledge and celebrate with each other. When this delight is experienced within the partnership on a regular basis, both of you will be drawn to continue the practice and spend more time with each other.

Celebration can be woven into every aspect of our practice, not just the joyful moments. We can applaud even the times of frustration or failure. In fact, those less-than-perfect moments can be seen as valuable steps on the path to success. In Acro, there are just as many moments of frustration as there are of delight, but those frustrations are part of what makes it such a rich experience. They're the little missteps that lead to breakthroughs and growth.

One way to shift how you relate to these moments is to reframe them as experiences worth celebrating too. For example, in the Salt Lake City Acro community, there was a practice of replacing "Sorry" with "Surprise!" whenever a skill didn't work out as planned. Instead of apologizing for a slip or a wobble, they'd simply say, "Surprise!," turning an unexpected fall into a moment of lightness and laughter. It's a gentle reminder that when things don't go as we expect, it's not something to blame or apologize for. When you allow room for failure, and stop seeing every attempt as needing to be perfect, you open up more space for creativity and experimentation. This creates a culture where mistakes are part of the fun and everyone can learn and grow together. So next time something doesn't quite work out, take a breath, smile, and let out a cheerful "Surprise!"; you're still moving forward.

Your partnership will have much more room for moments of enjoyment and growth when you both celebrate delight and frustration with a sense of gratitude. It will create a secure partnership that draws you closer together. You will foster a connection that feels less draining and more fulfilling for your inner selves.

> *"Standing hand to hand was something I dreamed of, but I was convinced it would never happen. It took me over a year of consistent training, with multiple teachers, including the authors of this book, and flyers willing to gift me reps to get there. The first time it happened was at the Chicago Center for Dynamic Circus in December 2023. I was at a skill-share jam with about 20 acrobats playing with all kinds of skills. I asked a seasoned hand to hand flyer if I could attempt one, and she cheerfully agreed. Then, for reasons I can't explain, it all clicked. It felt strong and quiet. I thought maybe it was just in my head, but the room actually fell silent as my Acro family watched. Hearing whispers of 'yeah dude' and 'hold it' made it real. After a few seconds, the flyer came down, and I was met with hugs and applause I'll never forget. To celebrate, I ordered deep dish pizza." –C.J, Chicago Acro Community*

The R in ACRO: Rituals and Routines

If the other parts of ACRO serve as the attractions and appetizing elements, then the rituals and routines serve as the structure and stabilizing elements of a secure relationship. The regularity of routines comforts the attachment system so that there is room for connections to be developed. People tend to prefer relationships that are reliable. They like environments where they know what to expect without jarring surprises. This also applies to each person's nervous system and sympathetic responses.

Building consistent routines with a partner can be a powerful way to create a sense of predictability and nurture a feeling of anticipation. In the context of an Acro partnership, for example, setting aside time to practice together at least once a week allows you to have space to grow your sense of attunement. The regularity lets you stay connected to what might be shifting for each of you, whether physically or emotionally. Routines become touchpoints that reinforce the shared expectations and commitments you've made. By showing up consistently, you send a clear message that the partnership you're both investing in is important and valued.

Rituals and routines both play important roles in our lives, but they hold different meanings, especially when it comes to relationships. Rituals are actions we choose to give extra attention and meaning to. Routines are repeated actions that become part of a system, often requiring less thought or emotional engagement over time. Think of brushing your teeth or your usual route to work, useful but automatic. Rituals carry a sense of intention, often marking something we find valuable or sacred. For example, having dinner with friends every Friday might be a routine. But if, once a month, that dinner includes a moment of reflection or celebration of your friendship. It becomes a ritual. That small shift in awareness can make the experience more meaningful. Rituals like these help strengthen relationships by actively recognizing the role someone plays in your life and the shared relationship you're building together.

The rituals you create and maintain together offer a foundation for how you'll treat each other and set the tone for your interactions. For example, you might have a warm-up routine that you always do together. Or maybe you make a habit of pausing to check in face-to-face before jumping into any physical practice. Starting each session with a simple authentic conversation, sharing how you're feeling that day, or mentioning anything that might be on your mind can help build trust and clarity in your partnership. You can also create small fun rituals around milestones, like having a special handshake or high five to celebrate when you finally pull off a challenging skill. These rituals, no matter how big or small, help strengthen your connection by making your shared moments feel more meaningful and grounded.

Creating time and space to be fully present with each other with a routine cadence, is an important part of helping your secure relationship flourish. In a world full of distractions and competing demands, the feeling of having someone's full attention is incredibly powerful. When you take the time to be with each other without the interruptions of your daily routines, focusing your attention on your partner and listening without rushing to respond can feed into the other person. These small yet meaningful acts of presence help each person feel truly seen, heard, and valued. They allow for a deeper understanding of each other's inner world, and they foster an environment where you can both feel safe to be yourselves. Over time, these moments build trust and emotional safety, reinforcing the foundation of your partnership.

As the time you spend together grows, it's important to intentionally maintain a sense of curiosity in your interactions. While your shared routines may become smoother and more automatic with practice, the connection between you shouldn't slip into autopilot. Even within familiar routines, it's helpful to stay engaged by bringing a playful or curious energy into your practice. This could look like playfully challenging yourselves with a new variation of a familiar movement, turning part of your routine into a game, or simply asking your partner how they might approach the routine if they were in your shoes. These moments don't have to disrupt your flow, they can be small additions that deepen your connection and help you see each other in new ways. They will keep your partnership fresh, engaged, and growing.

Routines can have a powerful effect on our state of mind and the versions of ourselves that we bring into a relationship. For instance, have you ever noticed how, when you're around old friends from high school, you find yourself slipping into a younger, more playful version of yourself? That's the impact of those familiar routines and shared memories shaping your present experience. In your Acro partnership, the routines you create together can also bring out certain parts of yourself. They might reveal a more focused, patient version of you, or allow for a more playful, adventurous side. By staying aware of how these routines influence you, you can invite the parts of yourself that feel most authentic and aligned with the secure, attuned partnership you're building together, to grow. *Are your routines reinforcing the dynamic you want to cultivate together, or are they bringing out behavioral patterns from other relationships or environments? Do they reflect how each of you is growing and evolving?* Periodically checking in on this can help ensure that your time together supports the most aligned and authentic version of your relationship.

The O in ACRO: Openness After Conflict

Disagreements and arguments are inevitable when practicing with others and trying new things. You'll experience the same moment as your partner, but from different perspectives, based on your past experiences and individual identity. The differences that come up may cause friction between you. When these conflicts in perception or opinion come up, it's not unhealthy to have an argument or non-physical fight with each other. The ability to come together after conflict is what helps the relationship grow and adds to its longevity. Coming back together after conflict enhances communication and builds more secure feelings toward each other and the relationship. We will cover some tools for respectful conflicts in Chapter 12. The supporting resources will provide much more information about conflicts and fights than we will cover in this book. We'll focus the remainder of this section on how disagreements can benefit the development of a more secure relationship with each other.

Having a difference of opinion or need that leads to an argument does not mean that there is a wound in the relationship. Conflict can be a normal and healthy aspect of a fulfilling relationship. It is part of the cycle of disruption and homeostasis that leads to growth and resilience. When learning a new skill in Acro, it takes both people's efforts to make the skill smooth and synced. Because each person may be doing different movements, their needs can also vary from moment to moment. When arguments about what should happen occur between you, they allow for clashing and resolution. Resolving conflict where both of you feel that the other person is not severing your connection to the relationship, reinforces that you will be there for each other in tough times and can depend on each other more.

Conflict often arises when there's a breakdown in attunement—when one or both people no longer feel seen, heard, or understood. At the heart of many disagreements is a simple but powerful human need: the desire to be acknowledged and sensed by those we're in relationship with. When that need isn't met, it can stir up feelings of disconnection, frustration, and hurt. That's why attunement, tuning in to each other's emotions, needs, and unspoken signals, is such a vital skill. When we feel truly seen by someone, even in moments of tension, it helps de-escalate conflict and strengthens the foundation of trust in the relationship. Being curious, checking in, and really listening can go a long way in restoring connection and preventing small misunderstandings from becoming big divides.

Conflict can feel painful, and during moments of pain, you may try to turn away from the things that are triggering the pain. When the source is your partner, turning away from them may feel like an attachment rupture for one or both of you. When this rupture persists for too long, it can jeopardize the sense of safety in the relationship and trust can be lost. To allow the rift in the connection to heal, you have to open yourself up to the other person. This opening up needs to happen in order for you to be understood, and to understand the why of the pain.

Being able to understand your partner's why, in their words, is a way to soothe the feeling of fear of an unknown element that has set off alerts in your nervous system. Turning toward your partner with genuine curiosity can be a powerful tool for deepening understanding and reducing defensiveness. It can help you move past conflict and find a shared sense of connection. But it's important to recognize that this level of vulnerability isn't always easy. It can feel safer and easier to blame or criticize your partner instead of taking the risk to share how you're really feeling. It can be powerful to lean into this vulnerability. It can open the door to more authentic conversations and a stronger, more trusting relationship.

During the repair phase of a conflict, it's important that each of you take responsibility for your own roles in the conflict. This has shown to build more security in the relationship. Research by John and Julia Gottman[2] found that people who are honest about their mistakes appear much more believable and trustworthy than people who try to defend themselves by deflecting blame. The principle of I/we communication can also be very effective in how each person handles conflict. In conflicts, it's not important that you say the right thing or are on the right side. It's very important that you're as genuine and considerate as you both can be in these moments.

As you and your partner embark on building a healthier and more secure relationship, the moments that you experience together will be more fulfilling and give you more of the things you need. Having a partnership that you feel secure about will give each of you more comfort in the hard times. Your security will imbue you both with a sense of stability when hard times of conflict arise in either other areas of your lives, or within the relationship. It will elevate the moments of elation and excitement when you find your ways back to a balance that celebrates you in ways that feel most appreciated. Incorporating the principles in this chapter into your relationship will give it more security in ways that can become second nature when using them together.

It may not always be simple to implement these principles in every attachment-based relationship you have. It will take intention and effort to work these things into your chosen relationships, but most of the time, it will be worthwhile. We will share additional tools and exercises in later chapters for when more challenging moments arise. As you both are building more fulfilling secure relationships with each other, It will also be important to develop your own secure relationship with yourselves. That's important so you can show up in your shared relationship with as much of your own self as possible in each moment.

The principles in this chapter can be applied to your own development, but with a little twist. We explore that more in the next chapter. We are very glad that you will be incorporating healthy dynamics into your relationships. We're aware of how that will likely impact your lives and, by extension, the lives of the people around you. The community will only get stronger as each individual member and relationship gets stronger and more secure.

Notes

1. *Daniel P. Brown and David S. Elliott, Attachment Disturbances in Adults: Treatment for Comprehensive Repair (New York: W. W. Norton, 2016).*
2. *Gottman and Silver, The Seven Principles for Making Marriage Work.*

11

ACRO on Your Own: Secure Attachment with Self

Acro is inherently a practice in which you're physically connected to one or more people. Nevertheless, it is significantly better when you have a strong relationship with yourself. An important value surrounding safety in Acro is accurate self-assessment. That means you can check in with yourself and judge whether you are ready to attempt a skill or not. It is important to confirm that you are mentally present, physically able, and emotionally focused. There are many valid reasons why you may not be ready in that moment, but a significant part of becoming more experienced is becoming more acclimated to when you are ready, and when you aren't. Being able to know yourself, acknowledging your own feelings, and having the self-esteem to stand up for your state of being are aligned with a secure attachment bond with yourself.

Even if you feel you didn't develop a secure attachment style as a child, you can still cultivate one as an adult. Developing a secure attachment style as an adult is called Earned Secure Attachment. We have discussed how to build secure attachment relationships with chosen people, but you can go a step deeper. You can develop your own secure attachment style in how you interact with both the world and yourself. You don't need to rely on secure attachments within particular relationships. We have discussed the ways you can be an example in your relationships for the behavior you want to see. You can also motivate others by building that model within yourself. Understanding what your ideal model of feelings and values are for yourself provides clarity about your aligned self, that is, the person you see as yourself in your best moments.

The aligned self is the version of you that acts in ways that are consistent with your values, needs, intentions, and deepest sense of truth. It is not a perfect version of yourself, but an attuned one. When you are aligned, your choices, reactions, and relationships more closely reflect who you want to be, rather than being driven mainly by fear, insecurity, pressure, or old survival patterns. When you become more rooted in your aligned self, you bring greater clarity, steadiness, and intention into your life and experiences. You are more able to make choices that reflect your values, rather than reacting only from fear, pressure, and habit.

In Acro, the aligned self has better boundaries, clearer communication, more accurate self-assessment, and a stronger capacity to participate from a place of trust and presence. Beyond Acro, living from your aligned self can shape the kinds of relationships you build, the opportunities you pursue, and the ways you respond to challenges. It can help you feel more grounded in who you are, less reactive to the expectations of others, and more able to create a life that feels honest, meaningful, and connected to your deeper intentions.

Go ACRO On Your Own

Taking on the idea of practicing Acro on your own can be approached from several different practices. You could train in gymnastics or acrobatics, develop a yoga practice, or focus on handstand training. It's pretty amazing how aligned a personal handstand practice can be with the journey that a person has in their Acro practice. The ways that you communicate with others are often exaggerated when speaking to yourself. The speed at which you move when training on your own is hard to shift away from significantly while training with another person. The principles you uphold in how you train in handstanding will strengthen the style of connection that you contribute to your partnerships. Some of the common principles used to improve handstands are awareness of self and body; moving isometrically, that is, without disrupting other parts of you; and facing frustration and imperfection. There are many lessons learned while developing a handstand practice that relate closely to developing a more secure attachment with yourself.

As you review the following principles of being AcroSecure within yourself, you will need a space to practice these principles. Depending on how you learn or engage with yourself, you can exercise these principles within a journaling practice, meditation, or while working on your handstand. It's most important to have a space where you can be present with yourself. While we won't be prescribing specific exercises for each of these practices in the text of this book, give yourself undivided attention, and track your progress in some way.

A in ACRO: Attuning to Yourself

Feeling comfortable in your own body allows you to express yourself more fully, stand your ground when disagreements occur, and push for growth opportunities. Feeling that comfort also allows you to find a better understanding of yourself and your needs, and to know when things are off-balance. Finding comfort in yourself is not always inherent for all of us. It can take effort to learn how to be comfortable with your own thoughts and presence. Just as it takes time to get used to another person, it may take intentional time to attune to your own inner world and the voice within you. Taking time to attune to the subtle signals and rhythms of yourself is about really noticing how you feel, what is happening within your physical body, and what you may need in the moment.

At first, you may not appreciate the thoughts you encounter when you are on your own. Do not turn away or find distractions from those thoughts. Stay with them and give your consciousness time to attune to all the things that are happening within you. There are many feelings that you can dive into within your mind and body, whether it is the physical sensations of your five senses, or the urges for hunger, desire, or longing. Checking in with yourself at various times and in many different situations will give you a more robust understanding of the common thoughts and sensations that are normally part of your personality. Knowing when you may be in a state that is outside that norm can give you signals to take action to get yourself back to a more ideal state of mind. Taking a walk on your own, or meditating can give space for diving into yourself while stepping away from your regular environment.

> *"I'll be honest. I definitely have commitment issues and can be a bit of a flight risk when a relationship feels unstable. But the opposite is true when the foundation is steady as a rock. My heart may have wanted certain outcomes, but I trust my head to make the same choices again. When I look back on the times I felt hesitant and let that guide my decisions, I don't feel like I missed out by pulling away. If anything, I feel like I was coming home to myself and to the wisdom of my intuition that brought me where I am today. I'm grateful for my secure relationship. My partner never makes me question his intentions or feelings, so I lean in. Whether a relationship is romantic or platonic, I don't hesitate to set boundaries or cut undeserving people out of my life. I don't lean into relationships that feel unsafe or insecure because life is too short and I value sustainability."*
> *–J.G. Austin Acro Community*

There are so many triggers that we encounter in the world each day. How we keep ourselves in a non-agitated state shows us how we can soothe ourselves. If we find we're often angry or anxious, we may struggle regulating our emotional state. A calm and regulated mind is essential to remaining non-defensive as we navigate various situations. There are several ways we can regulate our emotions and bring ourselves back to a calm and balanced state. These methods help us shift our focus, soothe our nervous system, and find a sense of stability during challenging moments. Whether we're practicing on our own, or within our partnerships, learning and using these regulation tools can make a significant difference.

The first way we tend to regulate ourselves is through auto-regulation. Our bodies and minds automatically take steps to soothe us in moments of distress. This happens without much conscious thought and can be triggered by both emotional and physical urges. Auto-regulation is something we do on our own, without needing others, and it can involve physical and mental strategies. Physical examples include nail-biting, rocking back and forth, and pacing. Mentally, it might involve daydreaming, zoning out with TV, or even using substances like alcohol or drugs to distract ourselves. These actions may help with self-soothing, but they do not contribute to self-attunement or building the awareness it takes to intentionally improve our emotional states.

Another method we use to soothe ourselves, which we learned as infants, is external regulation. This is when we turn to someone to help us calm down and find a sense of ease. As children, that person was usually a parent or caregiver. As adults, it's often a romantic partner, family member, or even a close friend. It can look like being held, hugged, or talking out your worries with someone you trust. In the context of Acro, external regulation can show up in the form of a Spotter, someone who can help you feel safer when attempting a skill. Even if they're not physically touching you, just knowing they're there can be comforting.

While external regulation can be incredibly helpful, it's also important not to rely on it too much. If we lean too heavily on others to regulate our feelings, it can hold us back from the growth that comes with learning how to soothe ourselves and understand our own emotions. Having someone there to support us while we sit with discomfort and find our balance can be a wonderful part of the process, but it's equally important to develop our own capacity for self-attunement and self-regulation.

The third method of regulation that's available to us, and one that's frequently used in Acro practices, is interactive regulation. With this method, both people co-regulate at the same time. They help each other find balance and calmness together. In Acro, this kind of regulation is crucial, because we move as a team and don't want to accidentally override or counteract each other's energy or balance. Interactive regulation can show up in small, powerful ways, like taking a deep breath together, giving a reassuring squeeze, or offering a few encouraging words while we're working through a skill. It's a beneficial method that requires us to stay aware of our own emotions and actions while at the same time tuning in to our partner's feedback. The more we're both in sync, the stronger and more secure our shared experience becomes.

Self-regulation is the last method of regulation we'll talk about, and it's one of the most important, especially as we work on developing secure attachment. It's a key part of feeling safe and grounded within ourselves. It also supports the security we can bring to our relationships. Consciously regulating our own emotional state helps us stay in our ideal state more consistently, and makes it easier to recover from moments when we feel overwhelmed or emotionally flooded. When we're in that calm, balanced place, we're able to make choices and take actions that feel true to who we are. Self-regulation means we get comfortable with being ourselves. It's beneficial to tune into what calms and soothes us even when we're around other people. Whether it's a calming thought, a grounding breath, or a comforting physical movement, discovering those self-soothing sensations are at the heart of self-regulation.

Putting self-regulation into practice can be done in many ways; it's all about finding what works for you. A popular tool is using breathing techniques, like square breathing. This is a calming method where you inhale, exhale, and hold your breath for equal intervals. It is a practice that can shift your focus away from overwhelming thoughts and bring your attention back to something steady and within your control: your breath. For example, in a handstand practice, focusing on your breath can isolate muscle engagement while minimizing disruptions from other parts of your body. Another helpful approach for self-regulation is using mantras that reaffirm your values or the state of mind you want to embody.

The strategies for attunement with yourself can be used in many ways, but attuning to yourself and recognizing when your actions aren't aligned with your ideal self is key. This awareness helps you know how to bring yourself back to a calmer, more enjoyable state of mind. Understanding your aligned self also lets you spot the things that might throw you off balance, so you can set healthy boundaries that keep you in a good space. Staying in a comfortable state of mind and moving toward the aligned version of yourself creates a headspace that feels genuinely good to be in. Good headspace will encourage a relationship with yourself that you will be excited to nurture.

C in ACRO: Celebrate and Enjoy Your Thoughts

Enjoying being with yourself can be a wholly fulfilling experience, especially when you are excited to see the positive parts of yourself appear. You can choose to create an outlook where your aligned self appears more often. It can be a good goal. You can work to encourage that part of yourself to show up more often by celebrating and rewarding the moments you're proud of. Take time to fully visualize who you see as your aligned self and how they will behave in significant moments. Understanding when you are being more like your aligned self, rather than other versions of yourself, will give you chances to reinforce that ideal version of you.

Being in your head can be a really enjoyable experience. After all, your thoughts are an influential part of how you experience the world. The way you speak internally has a powerful impact on your thoughts and emotional state. Improve your internal speech by shifting your inner dialogue toward more affirmative comments that focus on what you want, rather than what you're trying to avoid. The subconscious mind doesn't register words like not or instead, so if you focus on what you don't want, your mind might actually give more attention to those things. By intentionally focusing on your desires and goals, you're more likely to move in the direction you want to go.[1]

When you remember that your subconscious mind tends to focus on the messages you're giving it, it's easy to see how thoughts of self-criticism and shame can become even more powerful. By minimizing these negative thoughts and shifting your self-talk to something more positive and encouraging, you'll notice a positive impact on your mental well-being and enjoyment of life. One helpful strategy is to catch yourself the moment those thoughts begin and intentionally interrupt them. You can break this negative cycle with a physical action, like moving your body, changing your posture, or even with a vivid mental image. You can use a fun, catchy song to shift your mood. If interrupting these thoughts on your own feels difficult, consider asking a trusted friend to share some positive affirmations, or gently repeat what they're hearing you say so you can recognize which thoughts aren't serving you. It will make it easier to let them go. With practice, you'll build more control over your thought patterns and create space for a more positive, encouraging inner voice.

Celebrating yourself becomes even more powerful when you're intentional and specific about what you're honoring. Instead of a vague "good job," take a moment to name the exact accomplishment or meaningful experience, whether it was setting a boundary, showing up consistently, or making progress on something that's been challenging. When you clearly acknowledge what you did and why it matters to you, your mind is more likely to register the moment as meaningful and worth remembering.

To deepen the impact, try capturing these moments in a journal, voice note, or short video. This not only reinforces the memory but creates a personal archive you can revisit during tougher times when you need encouragement or a reminder of your growth. Celebrating yourself can also include small rituals: doing a happy dance, treating yourself to something enjoyable, or sharing your win with someone you trust. These acts of celebration, big or small, help anchor your self-worth, affirm your progress, and make joy an intentional part of your relationship with yourself. When celebration becomes a habit, it strengthens your confidence and nurtures a sense of pride in who you are becoming.

Give yourself rest not only as a reward for a job well done, but also as a gentle remedy for those moments of frustration when you're feeling emotionally off-balance. Sometimes the best thing you can do for yourself is pause and step away for a little while. Rest doesn't always mean sleeping or napping, it can also mean taking a quiet moment to breathe deeply, enjoy a comforting activity, or even just let your mind wander. By giving yourself these restful pauses, you're sending a powerful signal to your body and mind that it's okay to slow down and regroup. This simple act of kindness toward yourself can work wonders for resetting your energy. It will help you find a calmer, more centered place from which to move forward.

R in ACRO: Rituals and Routines for a Secure Self

The security you feel in yourself can be deeply influenced by how you treat yourself. Your nervous system benefits from predictability, because it creates a comforting sense of stability. Giving yourself structure, through rituals and routines, can help you build a solid foundation for your life. This could be in the form of a physical home, but it doesn't have to be. Having these stabilizing practices in your daily life can make it easier to explore new relationships and engage with the wider world. Routines help simplify your day by reducing the number of decisions you need to make, while rituals help you focus your attention on what truly matters to you and your aligned self.

Routines are a powerful tool for supporting your foundation. These repeated actions help simplify your daily choices and reduce the mental load; they free up energy for more meaningful activities. For example, when you brush your teeth and prepare meals at the same time each day, they become automatic, thereby creating a comforting rhythm. You can also use routines to reinforce self-worth by integrating self-care practices into your mornings and evenings. Such activities as gentle stretching, skincare, or even attentively cleaning your living space help you feel attuned to your life. These routines signal to your mind and body that your well-being matters. They lower emotional overwhelm and reinforce a sense of safety within. By making some daily choices into routines, decisions will be easier. You can also set up healthier choices for yourself, such as having a regular warm-up routine before exercise, consistent meal times, and a regular sleep schedule.

Creating routines for self-awareness can also strengthen the relationship you have with yourself. Setting aside daily or weekly check-ins allows you to notice what emotions you're experiencing in your body, or if there are unmet needs that deserve attention. These moments of self-attunement help nurture a sense of emotional safety. They're also a chance to see if your actions are aligned with your values and your ideal self. As long as you remain focused and avoid distractions, these check-ins can be not only productive but also enjoyable.

Rituals are another important aspect of this principle of a secure self. While similar to routines, rituals carry deeper intention and meaning. They help elevate everyday moments into something more sacred. For example, taking a moment to set an intention before a practice, or reflecting after a session, adds emotional weight to those experiences. Rituals signal to yourself that certain moments matter. They reinforce a sense of value and self-respect. Consider creating personal rituals for times of transition, like seasonal shifts or moving from work to play mode. Rituals can make these transitions smoother and more intentional.

It's also essential to include rest in the foundation of your secure self, not just as a reward, but as an active, restorative choice. Rest helps reset your nervous system and supports emotional regulation. Whether it's unplugging for quiet time, taking a walk, or simply allowing yourself to do nothing, intentional rest builds trust in yourself and prevents burnout. It's about giving your nervous system a break from constant external stimulation. Many people need to actively choose rest; it doesn't always come naturally. Giving yourself permission to pause is a powerful way to stay regulated and connected to your needs.

As you establish these rituals and routines, remember that

they don't have to feel rigid or unchanging. Monthly milestone rituals can prompt you to reassess and adjust your routines to align with your goals and growth. Routines can be dynamic and evolving if you allow them to be. Setting aside time to try new activities or revisit old ones can keep your days fresh and adventurous. Ask yourself how your aligned self would want to approach this next period of time. The ongoing flexibility will keep your relationship with yourself feeling alive, engaged, and attuned to who you're becoming.

Lastly, while rituals and routines provide stability, they shouldn't consume your autonomy. Routines should lighten your mental load, not weigh you down or feel like a chore. If you notice certain routines or rituals no longer feel supportive, ask yourself: *Are these practices helping me feel secure and aligned with who I want to be?* If there's a gap, adjust your rituals and routines to better reflect your evolving self. Your foundation should always support the most authentic version of you.

O in ACRO: Be Open After Inner Conflict

As you take steps toward your aligned self, there will be many moments in which you will encounter resistance and struggle to feel secure. You may not always act in the ways you think are ideal. When these moments come up, how you react and how you speak to yourself can make a significant difference between whether you are able to bounce back and build resilience, or if these moments become regrets that chip away at your self-image. By revisiting the moments where you felt you let your aligned self down, you can take steps to manage the triggers. You can learn to minimize the impact emotional triggers have on your daily life.

Reframing how you view your role in the situations where you acted in ways that you regret can change how those mistakes sit in your mind. In the work of Brené Brown,[2] how you frame your mistakes is the difference between shame and guilt. Shame is much more detrimental to your self-image than guilt. Recognizing when your mistakes are something that you have done (guilt), and not because of who you are (shame), can give your mind room to see how you might act in ways closer to your aligned self in future situations. How you talk to yourself during these troubling times shows you whether you speak with kindness or criticism. Be kind to yourself. Avoid calling yourself stupid, clumsy, or helpless. Lean into a positive perspective of your actions. Learn to recognize when negative self-talk comes up and what triggers are related. Building this awareness is one step toward learning to more fully accept yourself and your role in your personal situations.

Pay attention to the moments when you feel less in control of your emotions and reactions. Doing so can help you uncover your emotional triggers. Learning how to manage these triggers is an important skill for gaining more control over your emotional state. Start by noticing what tends to contribute to these moments of emotional reactivity. Determine what is occurring for you when you get into these states. Ask yourself, *what usually comes up for me in these situations?* Is there a story you tell yourself, or a particular feeling that becomes overwhelming? Common triggers might include feelings of rejection, unfair treatment, threats to having your needs met, and grief. To better understand their origins, you can also try digging deeper by thinking back to when you first experienced these feelings.

> *"Watching my partner play with other people during and after my past relationship trauma was hard, and it seeped into my analyzing my own skills and thinking that there was always a better Acro person simply because I was not being treated with personal respect." –J.H., Florida Acro Community*

Once you identify some of your triggers, you become more aware of situations that might bring them up. This awareness allows you to decide how you would rather feel and respond when similar situations arise in the future. While you may still get triggered at times, this awareness gives you more space and the option to choose your reaction. It can be similar to being in an intense situation with adrenaline, such as attempting a risky new skill. Each time you face it, you learn more, see more possibilities, and gain more control over how you respond. Each time, you get better at reacting in ways that feel right for you.

When you find yourself in the middle of a triggering situation, you can take steps with **trigger management** to actively move through these tough positions. Remember to recognize that you may be mentally hindered by an emotionally triggered state and accept that you still have choice and responsibility in the way you react. Try to understand what triggered the strong emotions. Then you can understand what you are reacting to. Work to choose what you would like to feel in this moment and what you want to do to move toward that desired outcome.

You can actively shift your emotional state by changing some of the factors in the situation. One important factor is your physical body. For example, you can move away from the situation that's triggering you, or focus on your breath to calm the tension in your body. Another factor you can influence is your mind. You can redirect your thoughts by focusing on a powerful memory or concept that brings you a sense of calm and strength. With practice, these steps will help you feel more in control of your reactions. While the feelings behind your triggers might never fully disappear, you can learn to prevent them from taking over your response in the moment.

In this modern era, it is important to be aware of the ways that we speak to ourselves and the situations that throw us off balance. Each of our lives are immensely complex. The many elements that influence us can have an impact on the thoughts that go through our minds. From the encroachment of social media in our social lives and the messaging we hear in modern media, to the events we hear about in the news, there are too many things that impact our thinking. Many of these come in ways that we may not be consciously aware of. In addition, there are many kinds of trauma that each of us may have endured that still sit with us at different levels of our identity. Knowing how to build a way to navigate the powerful elements that affect our emotional states of being gives each of us more mental space in which to make beneficial choices in our lives and the lives of the people we care about.

Notes

1. *James J. Gross, "Emotion Regulation: Affective, Cognitive, and Social Consequences," Psychophysiology 39, no. 3 (2002): 281–91.*
2. *Brené Brown, Dare to Lead: Brave Work. Tough Conversations. Whole Hearts. (New York: Random House, 2018).*

12

Spotting Techniques For Being AcroSecure

During challenging moments, even strong, secure relationships can feel unsteady. You might find yourself questioning the connection, feeling misunderstood, or unsure how to move forward. Emotions can run high. Frustration, sadness, or fear may surface, and communication may become strained. These moments can feel isolating, especially when the usual ways you and your partner connect no longer seem to work. It's common to feel overwhelmed, like you're speaking different languages, or like the bond you once relied on is out of reach. These are the times when doubt can creep in, not just about the relationship, but about your ability to handle the hardship together.

Keeping secure relationships healthy can take more than a strong foundation and consistent nurturing. It may take extra care. You may need new strategies to get through the hardest moments and make the repairs needed to move forward. Significant difficulties can take many forms, especially when they touch the places where trust, safety, and emotional security feel most vulnerable. In close relationships, these issues may include conflict that keeps repeating without resolution, jealousy that creates distance, feeling emotionally abandoned when support is most needed, or becoming so triggered that it is hard to stay open and attuned to one another.

In an Acro partnership, emotional strain can also build around moments such as one person feeling left behind as the other progresses more quickly, disappointment after a failed performance or training goal, feeling blamed after a drop or injury scare, struggling when one partner wants more intensity or commitment than the other, or feeling hurt when feedback lands as criticism instead of support. Even decisions about who to train with, how much time to spend together, or whether to continue teaching or performing as a pair can carry emotional weight. These are not small challenges, because they can affect both the relational bond and the sense of safety needed to practice well together.

Keeping Relationships Secure & Introducing New Partnerships

For some people, discovering a passion for Acro happens while they're already in a committed relationship. Unfortunately, sometimes their romantic partner does not share the same interest or choose to participate. This can create a natural shift, where attention and energy begin to grow in different directions. In a secure relationship, partners often support one another's exploration and growth, even when interests diverge. However, it's also normal for discomfort to arise, especially if one partner forms a close new platonic connection within the Acro community. This discomfort can stem from many places. Perhaps the new relationship feels threatening, or it starts to shift the balance of emotional fulfillment within the original relationship. These feelings don't necessarily mean something is wrong, but they do deserve attention and care.

Embarking on an Acro journey often sparks personal growth and shifts in identity. As you build confidence, learn new skills, and form meaningful connections, your sense of self will evolve. These changes can be empowering, but they may also create a gap between who you were when your relationship began and who you're becoming. For you or your partner, this shift can feel unsettling. When emotional distance or a gap in progressional growth begins to show, it can feel like an attachment rupture. In relationships with insecure attachment dynamics, this discomfort may trigger anxious or avoidant behaviors that create further tension. Taking time to reconnect and nurture the relationship during these periods of transition helps soothe the sense of disconnection before it deepens into something more wounding.

This growth can feel disorienting for either partner. When one person changes, it can create a sense of emotional distance. If left unaddressed, increasing time apart or directing significant energy toward outside people or interests, can start to erode trust, especially if you don't keep your partner informed. In relationships that are not securely grounded, this can feel like a threat. Without reassurance and open communication, your partner might interpret your involvement in Acro as a replacement or rejection. That's why it's essential to actively strengthen the emotional health of your existing relationship, particularly before introducing major new influences. Talk about your experience early and often, share your excitement, and include your partner in the journey where appropriate. Even if they don't join you physically in the practice, help them feel connected to your process; it will reduce anxiety and foster mutual respect.

Introducing a significant new relationship into your life can also bring up deeper questions about the structure and expectations of your current relationship. This is an opportunity, not necessarily a crisis, to revisit the foundations of your dynamic. You might find that your beliefs and desires don't fully align, and that's okay. Through open dialogue, you can explore how both partners' needs can be met, either within the relationship, with outside support, or through mutual compromise. Use the tools from Chapter 8; they can help you navigate this process with care. We recommend clear boundary-setting and non-defensive communication.

Finally, be mindful of how your time and energy are distributed. To those outside the Acro community, especially to partners and close friends, it might appear that Acro relationships are taking priority and disrupting their understanding of emotional security or relationship hierarchy. When these imbalances are left unspoken, trust can be damaged. To prevent this, it helps to be proactive. Prepare the relationship for upcoming changes by communicating openly. Share your feelings with care and reinforce your commitment to meeting each other's needs. Conflict, when handled with respect, can actually bring you closer. Jealousy doesn't have to be seen as a failure. It can be an invitation to engage with one another in more thoughtful, compassionate ways. Work together to reaffirm your commitment to the relationships that matter most. Healing and growth can coexist, but they need space for dialogue and intentional care.

Communicate Early and with Care

During transitions, communicating with care and intention is essential. Avoid assuming that past conversations still reflect your partner's current needs or expectations. Instead, check in with curiosity and compassion, asking questions like: "What feels important to you right now?" or "Has anything shifted in how you see our relationship or what you want from it?" These questions open the door to vulnerability and give each of you a chance to voice your truth with respect. One of the most important things you can do during this time is not taking for granted the meaning of the words and labels you've used in your relationship up to this point. Familiar terms like "exclusive," "affectionate," or even "committed" might seem clear on the surface, but underneath, they can carry different emotional weight or practical implications for each person.

To deepen your connection and prepare your relationship for the next stage, take time to individually, and jointly, unpack what these words actually mean to each of you. For example, both partners may say they value affection in the relationship, but one may define it as daily physical touch like hugging or holding hands, while the other might express affection through verbal affirmations before parting ways. Both are valid expressions of affection, but unless you clarify those meanings, you may unintentionally miss each other's emotional needs. Taking the time to understand these nuances can prevent future misunderstandings and help you both feel more seen and supported. For further exploration, The Five Love Languages by Gary Chapman can offer a shared framework for understanding the ways people express and receive love.[1]

It's also helpful to remember: don't compare your current relationship to someone else's, or judge your own dynamic based on past experiences. Comparing can lead to resentment, unrealistic expectations, and misplaced insecurities. Instead, focus on building your connection with honesty, curiosity, and compassion. Every relationship is unique, shaped by your individual histories, values, and communication styles. Bringing in outside standards can unintentionally create pressure or judgment. Stay focused on what works for the two of you in your current versions, and co-create a dynamic that reflects your shared values, not someone else's example.

Additionally, while close Acro partnerships can offer space for emotional support, be mindful not to lean on your Acro partner as a stand-in therapist for your romantic relationship. It can be tempting to process relationship struggles during long training sessions, especially with someone who feels emotionally safe. But over-reliance on that space can blur boundaries and unintentionally invite gossip, or create emotional entanglements. If you need to process challenges in your relationship, prioritize sharing your own experience rather than venting about your partner or others. Keeping the focus on self-awareness and responsible communication will help maintain the integrity of both your Acro and romantic partnerships.

How Attachment Pairings Shape Relationship Dynamics

One dynamic that can often show up in relationships is the "distancer-pursuer" pattern. In this dynamic, one partner, the distancer, habitually pulls away and seeks more space, while the other, the pursuer, tries to move in closer and bridge the gap. The more the distancer retreats, the more the pursuer chases, creating a cycle where neither partner's needs are truly met. This pattern is driven by underlying fears: the distancer fears being engulfed or losing themselves, while the pursuer fears being abandoned and left alone.

What often goes unnoticed is how the behaviors in this dynamic are shaped by subconscious patterns. The distancer tends to withdraw, creating space or shutting down emotionally when things feel overwhelming. This behavior often masks a deep fear of vulnerability, or being consumed by the relationship. Meanwhile, the pursuer tends to chase closeness, reaching out, demanding connection, or becoming increasingly anxious when that closeness isn't reciprocated. This pursuit can cover up an unacknowledged fear of being alone or abandoned. Ironically, each partner's behavior reinforces the other's reaction: the more one pulls away, the more the other pushes in. Rather than recognizing these behaviors as protective strategies, partners often focus on blaming each other, which prevents them from seeing the full picture or addressing the underlying needs at play.

To interrupt the distancer-pursuer pattern, both partners can practice self-awareness and intentionally shift their behaviors. For the pursuer, this might look like taking a step back and giving themselves permission to pause before moving in closer, allowing space for both partners to breathe. For the distancer, the work may involve leaning in: practicing vulnerability and sharing more openly, even if it feels uncomfortable. It's about disrupting the cycle by choosing small actions that are opposite to the usual pattern.

Another dynamic often seen in relationships is a fearfully anxious attachment dynamic, where a person feels uncomfortable or even terrified of being alone. They may develop patterns of promoting dependency, either by relying heavily on their partner or by making their partner dependent on them. This can include compulsive caretaking, not necessarily as a response to what their partner needs, but more as a strategy. The caretaker wants to keep the relationship feeling necessary to their partner in order to ward off their fears of abandonment. Even though people with this style tend to sacrifice themselves for the relationship, the ways in which they are anxious and compulsively give care are not necessarily attuned. If they sense any sign of distance, they may become demanding or possessive, seeking reassurance, connection, and even heightened emotional intensity.

For partners of someone with a fearfully anxious style, these needs can feel overwhelming or even insatiable. Despite the preoccupied person's genuine devotion, their behaviors can inadvertently push their partner away, creating the very disconnection they fear most. Research studies suggest that people with anxious attachment style behaviors, compared to people with a more secure attachment style, often experience more relationship conflict and jealousy, and may even struggle with ambivalence about their own intimacy choices, engaging in behaviors they don't truly want as a way to secure closeness.[2]

In the fearfully anxious dynamic, the anxious partner could find a better balance by focusing on nurturing their own sense of security and self-worth outside of the relationship. They could potentially move beyond their partner's validation through hobbies, friendships, or self-care practices that affirm their value. Rather than seeking constant reassurance, they could also practice self-soothing and create rituals that reinforce their independence. In both dynamics, open communication is key: naming the fears driving the behavior can help both partners understand what's really at play and find healthier ways to meet their needs.

How to Approach Jealousy When it Arises

Jealousy is a natural and deeply human emotion that nearly everyone experiences at some point in their relationships. It often arises when something we value, like attention, affection, or closeness, feels threatened or diminished. While jealousy is frequently portrayed as something negative or shameful, it can actually serve as a helpful signal that points to underlying needs, or insecurities that deserve attention. Instead of suppressing or judging these feelings, it's healthier to acknowledge them with curiosity and compassion. When approached with openness, jealousy can offer an opportunity for growth, deeper understanding, and stronger connections within our relationships.

As noted by Joli Hamilton, jealousy is a healthy and common human emotion.[3] Instead of feeling ashamed of our jealousy it's better to acknowledge it and sit with the feeling. In her research, Hamilton noticed that people who handle jealousy well tend to acknowledge their jealousy and don't judge it as a bad feeling. Instead, they normalize the emotion and remember that they can ask for what they need: reassurance, affection, or quality time with their partner. There are many reasons why jealousy may arise within each person in a relationship. While we won't cover all of these reasons, we do want to acknowledge that there is nothing wrong with these feelings coming up, even within a secure relationship.

Once feelings of jealousy are acknowledged, there can be space to explore which needs are feeling unmet, or where one person is experiencing a sense of lack. The sense of lack can be felt in any one of the many different needs a person has, such as fun, connection, attention, safety, quality time, and affection. And it can be expressed in different ways, including jealousy. Sometimes these feelings come up and are not immediately noticed. They may build up to a point where they are noticeable, and may take more effort to communicate and also reconcile. Being a partner who gives space for these emotions to be expressed can be healing for the person experiencing the feelings, and restorative for the relationship.

Working through this process the first few times can be jarring and feel antagonistic. As the two of you gain practice going through the process, both of you will be able to recognize and communicate the feelings and needs sooner after they arise. This will allow for reconciliation that does not take as much stress to resolve.

Compersion and Enjoying Other's Joy

Compersion is the feeling of genuine joy when someone else experiences happiness, success, or connection, especially when it's someone you care about. If you've ever felt excited when a friend lands a new job, or warm inside when your partner lights up talking about their day, you've already had a taste of compersion. This sense of shared joy can deepen emotional connections and, according to a study by Rhonda Balzarini, is even linked to greater relationship satisfaction.[4] One path to recognizing compersion is by acknowledging jealousy as a step to nurturing compersion. Every situation that might trigger jealousy, like your partner's close friendships or life wins, is also an opportunity to practice compersion instead. It's a learnable emotion, and one that can help create more secure, trusting, and joyful relationships.

Building compersion often starts by simply noticing it in everyday moments. Jodi Hamilton, who studies emotional experiences in relationships, recommends beginning with non-romantic situations.[3] Pay attention to those warm, expansive feelings you get when a friend reaches a milestone or does something they love, and name it. Noticing the physical sensations, like warmth in the chest or a softening of the shoulders, can help you become more aware of what joy for others feels like in your body. You don't need to eliminate jealousy to feel compersion. Jealousy and compersion can exist side by side. Letting yourself feel both can actually bring more depth, balance, and care to your connections. With curiosity and practice, compersion can become a more familiar and accessible part of your emotional landscape, enriching both your romantic and non-romantic relationships.

Navigating Conflict and Friction Healthily

Conflict is a natural part of any close relationship, and Acro partnerships are no exception. Sharing physical space, emotional energy, and personal goals with someone can bring about friction. But this isn't a sign that something is harmful. In fact, conflict often signals that both partners are engaged and invested. When approached with care and curiosity, disagreements can become valuable opportunities for growth. They help reveal unmet needs, differing perspectives, and unspoken expectations that, once acknowledged, can bring partners into deeper alignment.

In a productive Acro partnership, conflict can actually strengthen the bond between practitioners. The process of navigating tension, expressing vulnerability, and working through misunderstandings fosters trust, resilience, and clearer communication. Just like refining a skill through repetition and feedback, learning how to move through emotional challenges together builds a stronger, more adaptable connection. When both partners are committed to understanding, rather than winning, conflict becomes less about who is right and more about how to move forward together, with more insight, empathy, and mutual support.

While there are many teachings within the Acro community about communication and problem-solving, such as non-violent communication, using I instead of you, and others mentioned earlier in this book, a framework with similar values was developed by the Gottmans', which is covered in Chapter 6. Coincidentally, the mnemonic for the framework is aligned with other principles we are focusing on in this book. Their framework for navigating conflict is labeled "ATTUNE," which is where they state that conflict is caused by a lack of attunement between partners.

A *Awareness - choose words mindfully*

T *Tolerance - multiple ideas can be valid*

T *Transform criticism into wishes - wants over blame*

U *Understanding - no need for action yet*

N *Non-defensive listening - remain as calm as possible*

E *Empathy - don't try and fix your partner*

The first three responsibilities relate to the person speaking, whereas the last three relate to the person listening. Remain intentional in your expression while speaking during conflict. Remember that both of you are on the same team when sharing your concerns and needs. As the listener, it is even more important, and possibly tougher, to embody listening to connect. Work to not be defensive. To gain a deeper understanding of each of these responsibilities and the ATTUNE model, check out the work by John Gottman and Nan Silver.[5]

Expanding on the principles of ATTUNE within your Acro practice, one of the lessons that often emerges as you deepen your practice is the importance of co-regulation in shared movement. While refining techniques is valuable, the real breakthroughs in skill success often come from how well partners are able to regulate together emotionally and physically. After an unsuccessful attempt, the process of checking in, listening, validating, and adjusting calms the nervous system and strengthens the partnership. This mutual regulation builds trust and presence, which are critical foundations for progressing successfully in future attempts.

In fact, the improvements seen after a few failed tries are often less impacted by the immediate technical adjustments made, and more about the increased attunement between partners. Since motor learning requires repetition over time, technique rarely changes drastically between single attempts. What does shift quickly is how partners relate to each other. By becoming more receptive, more attuned to one another's signals, and more connected in their shared effort, the process of co-regulation allows true progress in Acro to unfold.

Learning to avoid, soften, or move out of defensiveness during conflict is not easy. It often requires significant self-work, including the kinds of practices discussed in Chapter 6, so you are less likely to be flooded by the intensity of the moment. In these situations, you may need to rely on your capacity for self-regulation, especially when your partner is not able to co-regulate with you. The person who is able to return to a calmer state first may be better positioned to lower their defenses and reach toward connection. As you speak with your partner, it is important to pay attention to how you are engaging. The way you communicate can either deepen the cycle of defensiveness or help create a path back toward understanding and reconnection.

To shift out of defensiveness, focus on your shared goal: understanding and resolution. Try validating your partner's perspective and look for something, no matter how small, you can take responsibility for. This diffuses tension and invites collaboration. As you communicate, highlight the parts of their experience that make sense to you and acknowledge any impact you've had. Even as you express your own view, let go of the need to be "right," and instead, prioritize finding a way forward. Ask what each of you can do to improve the situation. The ability to rebound from conflict and return to constructive dialogue is a strong indicator of emotional regulation and resilience in a partnership.

Even if you've made meaningful changes in yourself and your behavior, your partner may not immediately respond to those improvements. If they are still feeling triggered or emotionally activated, they might still be reacting to the relationship's unresolved tension, or the state it was in before or during the conflict. In some cases, it may take a conscious reset or renewal of the relationship dynamic before your partner can fully recognize and respond to the updated version of you.

When repeated arguments arise about what you and your partner should be doing during practice, or where to train, it may be a sign that your individual desires and expectations are beginning to diverge. This can be a natural part of growth within a partnership. To navigate these changes, it's important to have an open conversation where each of you can share your evolving goals and needs. This discussion can help you realign and intentionally renew your partnership dynamic to support the next phase of your shared journey.

Relationship Renewal

Relationships, like anything meaningful in life, need to be updated and renewed as the people in them grow and evolve. It's natural for each person to change over time. Our needs, values, goals, and even the way we express love, can shift as we gain new experiences or move through different life stages. But the relationship itself doesn't automatically adapt to those changes. Without conscious effort, they tend to stay frozen in the dynamics, habits, and assumptions that were present when they were last "defined." That's why relationships can start to feel out of sync or stuck. Not because something is wrong, but because they haven't been recalibrated to reflect who each person is now.

To keep a relationship aligned and thriving, it's important to regularly check in and intentionally update how you relate to one another. This can be as simple as setting aside time every few weeks or months to talk about what's working, what feels different, and what might need adjusting. Think of it as a shared ritual of renewal. A ritual of opportunity to explore how each of you is growing and how the relationship can grow with you. Ask questions like, “What do we each need now that we didn’t before?” or “Are there any ways our connection could feel more supportive or fun?” These check-ins don’t have to be heavy. They can be grounded in curiosity and care. By creating space for honest reflection and mutual growth, you give the relationship a chance to evolve with you, rather than hold you back.

Building awareness around how your own emotional patterns show up in your relationships can be a powerful tool for resilience. When partners take the time to reflect on what is being triggered in difficult moments, and approach those triggers with compassion and curiosity, they create space for healing, rather than harm. By recognizing the deeper roots of reactivity, both partners can begin to shift from defensive or avoidant patterns toward more open and empathetic communication. This not only helps navigate current challenges but also strengthens the foundation of trust and understanding moving forward.

Addressing these patterns doesn't require perfection. It requires presence, patience, and a willingness to grow together. Over time, even the most painful conflicts can become turning points that deepen connection, rather than tear it apart. By facing hardships with intention and care, partners can transform moments of disconnection into opportunities for repair, clarity, and renewed commitment. The journey of growth within a relationship is rarely linear, but it is one of the most meaningful investments you can make.

Notes

1. *Gary Chapman, The Five Love Languages.*
2. *David J. Wallin, Attachment in Psychotherapy (New York: Guilford Press, 2007).*
3. *Joli Hamilton, Nicholas R. Morrison, and Ayla N. Gioia, "Jealousy: A Comparison of Monogamous and Consensually Non-Monogamous Women's Experience," Cogent Mental Health 3, no. 1 (2024): 2283006.*
4. *Rachel N. Balzarini et al., "Compersion: When Jealousy-Inducing Situations Don't (Just) Induce Jealousy," Archives of Sexual Behavior 50, no. 4 (2021): 1311–24.*
5. *Gottman and Silver, The Seven Principles for Making Marriage Work.*

13

Acro Relationships and Dealing with Past Trauma

Acro offers more than just movement. It provides a living, breathing space for healing. By blending physical connection with trust-based communication, Acro creates opportunities to gently explore the patterns shaped by past trauma. In a society where emotional safety can be hard to find, the practice serves as a unique container where healthy relational dynamics can be tried out, experienced, and embodied. Whether through learning to support others or allowing yourself to be supported, Acro allows you to interact with old beliefs in new ways. Each posture or transition becomes a small but meaningful chance to interrupt ingrained habits and rewire your nervous system toward connection, stability, and trust.

In this process, the people you meet and move with can become **secure bases**, offering both emotional and physical grounding while you explore vulnerability, identity, and growth. The community environment can act as a **safe haven**: a place where it's okay to be seen, to fail, to ask for help, and to be your full self without judgment. For those who have felt unseen or silenced in other areas of life, Acro opens a new channel of expression. It holds space not just for physical play, but for personal reinvention. It invites each person to build a new relationship with their body, their emotions, and their sense of belonging.

Healing attachment wounds is essential because they shape how we move through the world and relate to others. When old wounds remain unaddressed, they can show up as difficulty trusting, chronic self-doubt, or a sense of disconnection in our most intimate relationships. Acro's ability to provide repeated, safe experiences of support and connection helps rewire these patterns by offering new models of how we can be in relationship with others. Each time we learn to receive support, trust our partner, and honor our own needs, we strengthen our capacity for healthy attachment, an essential foundation for thriving in every aspect of life.

> *"Ladies and Gentlemen, please meet my old friend, imposter syndrome. It's always blown my mind how much others believe in me to accomplish new skills when I don't see it in myself. Acro is special because it gives us a safe space to identify barriers and then have a community lift us up as we attempt to break through. No wonder this is such an emotional roller coaster for some. I mean, we're working out years of trauma and self doubt, brought on by a confusing and unfair world, and doing so through a positive practice. What's crazy to me is that even in the face of all*

this personal and Acro growth, I still have these moments where I'm like "I can't do that." –C.J., Chicago Acro Community

Triggers and Dynamics Common in Acro Communities

While there are many positive healing opportunities in the Acro practice, there are also many triggers and dynamics that can inflame past wounds or beliefs. It can be helpful to be aware of some of the more common triggering situations, and to know that you are not alone in experiencing them.

When practicing in environments where there are not as many established partnerships, finding people to play with can be an in-the-moment choice based on little information. In these moments, conscious or subconscious biases can factor into the decision making and cause a person to choose carelessly. They may inadvertently make a choice that doesn't mesh with their values and aligned self. These biases can be based on experiences they have had within their Acro journey, or from beliefs they gained outside of the practice itself. Common biases that come up in Acro interactions can be related to body size, visible personality attributes, and attractiveness. If a person repeatedly encounters difficulty finding responsive connections due to these biases, it can trigger previous attachment wounds or even create new ones that need to be addressed.

Body size can seem like an important consideration when imagining lifting a person above your own body. But when using proper technique, body size becomes a minimized factor. When approaching skills with solid technique, a 120 lb person can support a 220lb person with ease. Within society, this does not completely eliminate the idea that it would be easier to do a skill with a stronger person lifting a lighter person. There are stereotypes around who would make a better Base or Flyer, and who would be a person to choose as a partner to achieve certain skills. Stereotypes about basing often suggest that the role belongs to people with taller or larger bodies, greater visible strength, more masculine features, or louder, more dominant personalities. For Flyers, the stereotype often assumes the role is best suited to people with smaller, lighter bodies, more bubbly personalities, greater submissiveness, willingness to take instruction, and an appearance that fits conventional ideas of who should be seen and highlighted. None of these elements are true or based on factual reasoning, but come from conceptions of role models in media and the wider society.

Extending the ideas for who make more appealing Bases or Flyers are the visible attributes of personality, which can contribute to those stereotypes. Bases with louder voices and personalities tend to get approached more often and asked to play. Conversely, Flyers who have smiling bubbly personalities and are more outgoing tend to be engaged in more interactions and can ask for the things they want. Within this kind of dynamic, people with less outgoing personalities tend to get overlooked and left out more often. The people willing to engage others and ask for what they want, are able to get more attention and opportunities to play or train. Depending on the local community, elements of these biases can be more or less evident.

For people who frequently encounter the negative effects of bias, their sense of belonging within a community, and even their self-image, can be deeply impacted. Feeling that their presence or contributions are undervalued can be emotionally damaging. While behavioral strategies, like smiling first, or proactively asking to participate, might improve some outcomes, they don't necessarily heal the underlying wounds triggered by these interactions. True healing requires a shift in narrative or perspective. When feelings of exclusion arise, directly asking those involved why they didn't engage or include you can reveal their actual reasons, or their unawareness. This kind of honest dialogue can help challenge assumptions, clarify misunderstandings, and offer a more grounded and compassionate understanding of the situation. And this can support a healthier, more resilient internal narrative.

> *"I was always comparing myself to others. They seemed better, smaller, lighter, prettier, more flexible, stronger, more popular than me. My old partner would constantly choose other people to play with over me, and it reinforced those insecurities. It pushed me to try to be the best Flyer possible so I would get picked. Constant pressure on myself. I think if we could have talked it through and explored options, some of my needs might have been met, and it could have helped me work on those insecurities." –D.C., Oregon Acro Community*

To help heal these wounds, we each have a role in fostering a healthier community environment. This can start with something as simple as becoming aware of our own patterns, like who we tend to play with most often. It can start with setting intentional boundaries around how and why we choose our partners. In each practice space, teachers, community leaders, and "jambassadors" can also play vital roles by actively encouraging opportunities for everyone in the room to participate. Creating more positive, inclusive experiences helps counteract negative narratives and supports the healing of attachment wounds. Embracing community values like inclusivity requires more than just being welcoming. It means intentionally creating opportunities for everyone to grow, connect, and enjoy.

Power Dynamics in Communities

There can also be inherent power dynamics within certain communities that we should each be aware of. The influence that certain people in the community can have within interactions should not be ignored. The decisions that a teacher makes during a class, or outside of it, carry more weight than students. The lessons that a teacher shares in class ripple through the community. Additionally, the skills that they practice on their own while in a training space also creates interest in those skills within the community. Their example sets a standard, especially when choosing whether or not to use Spotters while training in community spaces. Teachers may not need to use Spotters for their own safety, but their students may take after their example leading to fewer people choosing to use Spotters, even if they may need them for safety. Teachers and students both play a role in shaping community culture, and the way each person acts can set an example for others throughout that space.

Another power dynamic often rooted in stereotypes is the assumption that Bases have more influence during a skill and, therefore, should hold more influence within the community. While both of these assumptions are false, they can still shape dynamics in certain spaces. This can lead to situations where Bases frequently share suggestions, while Flyer feedback is minimized or overlooked. When this pattern becomes normalized, it creates imbalances in communication and collaboration. Ignoring Flyers'input means missing out on half of the insight needed to improve a skill, or navigate a situation. Flyers bring a unique and essential perspective that can help complete the picture, leading to better solutions and more effective partnerships. For a community to thrive, it's crucial in every interaction to create space for all voices to be heard, respected, and valued.

A less often discussed power dynamic in some Acro communities is the influence of those who attend festivals or large events. In Acro, where there's often excitement around novelty, individuals who return from a festival with new skills or techniques tend to receive heightened attention and admiration. Along with those skills, they may also introduce new ideas or approaches, some of which may challenge or contradict existing teachings within the community. This can create tension, especially between those bringing in new concepts and established teachers who have invested time and identity in their methods. When new ideas appear to invalidate previous teachings, it may lead to discomfort or defensiveness. To maintain a healthy and collaborative community dynamic, it's important to recognize that there are often multiple valid ways to achieve the same outcome. Embracing new perspectives doesn't have to diminish the value of previous ones. Instead, they can expand the community's collective understanding and foster mutual respect among all contributors.

Dealing with Sexual Advances and Pressures

Within the heightened emotional and physical states that naturally arise in Acro, a wide range of feelings can surface as we move, play, and connect with others. The environment of Acro encourages deep interpersonal connection to achieve collaborative, playful feats, which can foster strong feelings of closeness. However, these feelings of connection can sometimes be misinterpreted as sexual attraction. It's not uncommon for some participants to assume that enthusiastic engagement or physical closeness implies romantic or sexual interest, but this is a misconception. Emotional connection and physical playfulness are not inherently sexual. It's important that communities do not normalize this assumption as a default pathway to intimacy.

When sexual or romantic feelings do arise, it's crucial to handle them with care, honesty, and respect. If appropriate and consensual, these feelings can be discussed openly using the principles and communication strategies outlined in Chapter 8. These conversations can help clarify boundaries, establish mutual understanding, and determine if there is space for those feelings to be reciprocated. If they are not, expressing awareness of your feelings and clearly stating that you will not act on them can create trust and help maintain a respectful dynamic going forward.

In building safe and inclusive communities, it's essential that we protect the trust people place in the moments when they choose to be open and vulnerable. Pressuring someone into a dynamic they haven't explicitly consented to, no matter how well-intentioned, can be a betrayal of that trust. This is especially important in environments like Acro, where physical proximity and shared vulnerability are integral to the practice. When someone is physically supported or emotionally seen in this space, they may feel especially raw and tender, and any violation of their boundaries can have a lasting impact.

Creating a safe environment requires not only explicit conversations about consent, but also an ongoing awareness of the subtle ways power dynamics and expectations can creep in. It means recognizing that even seemingly small gestures, like persistent suggestions, lingering touches, or repeated invitations, can feel like pressure to someone who is unsure how to say no. It also requires us to recognize that consent isn't just a checkbox; it's a continuous conversation that must be reaffirmed over time as circumstances and feelings shift.

By practicing this level of mindfulness, we create a culture where people can engage in Acro without fear of coercion, manipulation, or misunderstanding. We ensure that everyone, regardless of their level of experience, identity, or previous trauma, feels seen, respected, safe, and empowered to express themselves fully. In this way, we collectively foster an environment that can be a sanctuary for healing and growth, rather than another site of harm or confusion.

How Acro Supports Healing in Attachment and Trauma

Self Level

The potential of Acro to impact our personal journeys and heal the wounds that have shaped our sense of self is profound. Traumas, particularly those tied to decisions we believed we had control over, can damage our internal sense of safety and trust. This may affect our ability to regulate emotions, make calm decisions, or feel at home in our own bodies. This internal rupture can lead to feelings of inauthenticity. It can also make us feel misaligned with our values.

The practice of Acro inherently teaches each of us how to lean into situations where we have to consciously engage. Acro creates opportunities to mindfully engage with ourselves and others in real time. It asks us to navigate movements thoughtfully and find stability within partnership. This practice offers a safe environment to experiment with decisions and observe the immediate outcomes. Through repeated opportunities to try, adapt, and try again, we begin to build trust in our decision-making and grow confidence in what our bodies and minds are capable of.

Learning to trust ourselves requires experiencing both success and failure. Acro exposes us to a range of experiences that help us become familiar with the fears and other emotions that arise around failure. Failure helps us face and process the emotions we associate with not getting it right. Through this, we become more familiar with our fears, and less paralyzed by them. Experiencing failure in a space that doesn't cause harm to ourselves or others, helps rewire our internal responses. It begins to neutralize the emotional intensity of past traumas and creates a safer internal environment in which those wounds can eventually be addressed.

If self-trust or meeting your own needs feels difficult, learning to support others can be a valuable entry point. In Acro, we learn how to physically support another person's full weight and tend to their emotional states in real time. To do this, we must regulate ourselves, remaining calm and steady so we don't disrupt the alignment or connection. This attentiveness to another's physical and verbal cues teaches us to also notice the signals from our own bodies.

By practicing this awareness with others, we improve our ability to respond to our own physical and emotional needs with the same care. These skills help us tune into our own needs and the physical echoes of past wounds. Over time, this practice of listening and responding to others teaches us to listen more deeply to ourselves. Rebuilding trust in our decisions and learning to meet our own needs can strengthen our belief in what we're capable of.

The playful nature of Acro invites a shift in our internal dialogue. Here, failures aren't condemned; instead, we practice withholding judgment until it's truly helpful. One helpful practice shared by teacher Lux Sternstein is: "The first three don't count."[1] In other words, when learning a new skill, or revisiting one for the first time in a session, give yourself three attempts without judgment or feedback. These first attempts are for calibration, that is, they give you time to feel how your body is responding before evaluating outcomes.

Applied inwardly, this practice invites us to notice our thoughts without immediately labeling them as good or bad. When a particular thought returns three times, that repetition can signal something worth paying attention to. This gives our minds room to process without becoming overwhelmed by every passing emotion or idea, allowing clarity to emerge gradually. In this way, Acro becomes a path back to internal connection, resilience, and self-trust.

Relationship Level

The connections experienced through Acro have the potential to heal many of the relational traumas we carry from past experiences. Such traumas, like neglect, abandonment, betrayal, or inconsistency, can create deep attachment wounds and impact how we navigate connection and vulnerability. They can make it difficult to trust, to feel emotionally safe, or to allow intimacy and closeness. In some cases, these wounds stem from emotional or physical abuse that also needs attention and healing. For those who have experienced such trauma, or long-term patterns of relational harm, the challenge of forming safe, intimate connections can feel daunting.

In the early stages of an Acro practice, the inherently playful and collaborative nature of the discipline begins to gently reintroduce connection. Initially, this connection may be purely physical, as you are asked to share your weight and rely on another person's support. This requires trust and, often, a willingness to relinquish control. It can be difficult for people carrying relational trauma to be this vulnerable, especially in introductory classes. However, as you practice giving and sharing control, you begin to see that the support you long for can be offered and received unconditionally. You learn that you can remain comfortably suspended with minimal effort. Your partner is supporting you, not because of what you're doing, but simply because of your shared connection. This experience of unconditional support can feel foreign at first, but can be deeply healing. It challenges and disrupts old beliefs that you must control relationships, or earn connection in order to have your needs met.

When we open ourselves to the idea that relationships do not have to be conditional or transactional, we create space for support to be received without needing to immediately give back. Receiving becomes its own practice, no longer tied to the act of giving. Many people struggle with this. For example, they feel a compelling urge to return a compliment rather than simply accepting it with gratitude. In Acro, this is often practiced through spotting. For example, someone may be asked to spot during a session without assurance that they will get a turn to base or fly. When you learn to receive without expectation, you become more able to ask for and accept help during your low moments, even when you have little to give in return. Likewise, learning to give without expecting anything back can also be a powerful and healing shift.

As these beliefs about unconditional support begin to take root, we can also start to heal wounds around touch itself. For individuals with a history of **aversion to touch**, particularly those healing from physical violations, Acro offers a structured, consent-based environment with repeated, gentle exposure to non-threatening and caring touch. The repeated experience of being intentionally touched without threat or expectation, can rewire associations and soften the triggers that remain from past trauma.

> *"Growing up, I wasn't accustomed to touch very much. Even though my Mom was a hugger, the rest of my family wasn't. I didn't have that many opportunities to have prolonged touch all the way through school, including college. This left me feeling uncomfortable asking for or receiving touch unless I was very familiar with them. I mentally knew that touch was a good thing, but I was used to getting very little touch in my daily life. When I started doing Acro, this changed significantly. I allowed touch to happen in order to accomplish the skill, but it was during the downtime and friendly conversations that I learned to enjoy touch and also feel what it was like to have enough touch to be satisfied and nourished. It brightened my outlook on my daily experiences and added a whole new dimension to my close relationships."—Eric McKeethen, Co-author of this book.*

One particularly powerful component of Acro is its Thai massage element, which centers around the concept of healing touch. In this practice, touch is not only safe but intentionally nurturing. The giver attunes to the receiver's body, providing comfort, calming presence, and physical relief without asking for anything in return. The receiver must be open to vulnerability, primarily physical, but often emotional as well. This kind of touch is caring and intimate without any sexual expectation and allows the receiver to experience intimacy that is restorative rather than exploitative. For those with attachment styles primed toward anxiety or avoidance, healing touch can support the rebuilding of a foundation of safety and calm.

Acro also presents opportunities to re-establish how we connect in a modern world where social interactions are often driven by digital communication or substance-fueled environments.[2] Within the Acro community, connection is offered in the form of playful, intentional movement. The depth of the connection can be as limited or as meaningful as the person practicing desires. There is space for intimacy that isn't sexual, for interaction that isn't performative, and for belonging that isn't dependent on transactions. These experiences can provide a template for healthier relational bonds and help build trust, not only in others, but also in ourselves and in our capacity to relate with openness and safety.

Home Level

The experience that many people find within their local Acro community can feel a lot like a family. While it's true that some of these interactions can occasionally stir up past wounds, they also offer the potential to heal those same wounds, especially for those carrying deep attachment injuries from childhood and family life. For anyone who grew up feeling emotionally unsafe, excluded, or unsupported at home, being part of a community that values physical and emotional safety can help shift long-standing beliefs about what it means to feel safe in their environment.

Acro spaces are naturally collaborative and built around shared interactions. While there may be teachers or facilitators to help guide the space and ensure no one feels left out, each person has a great deal of autonomy. You get to decide how you engage, who you connect with, and how much you want to contribute to the energy of the group. For people healing from chaotic or neglectful family environments, this can be a powerful way to reclaim agency. You get to experience having a say in where and how you feel safe, seen, and supported. This sense of autonomy is a key part of healing. You're given the chance to actively create and reinforce the kind of environment that feels really safe and supportive for you.

As you find yourself leaning into the group dynamic, you may discover that this is a place where you can offer support to others and receive it in return without adhering to a set of conditions or family roles. It invites you to co-create safe, welcoming spaces where you are valued where you are. Over time, many people find that they're able to build a new sense of "home" through these connections.

Engaging with the diverse group of people in an Acro community opens your eyes to new perspectives. You might hear stories from others about how they grew up, what family means to them, or how they've navigated their own relationships to home and belonging. Importantly, you also begin to realize that family isn't just something you're born into. It can be something you create. Support, care, laughter, and consistency don't have to come from traditional family structures. Many people find that close friendships in communities like Acro, or even solo practices of self-care and self-trust can fulfill the roles that family once didn't. You get to choose who feels like home to you.

These insights can help you reframe your own story and recognize that family can take many forms beyond the one you were born into. It can also be something you intentionally build: a network of relationships that align with your needs, values, and hopes. Whether that family includes your current family, old friends, new friends, or even the Acro community itself, you have the power to choose the people and spaces that feel like home to you.

Community and Societal (Cultural) Level

Healing the wounds caused by community or societal harm can be subtle and complex. These wounds might not always be obvious, but their effects, such as anxiety, avoidance, and chronic insecurity, can run deep. Whether it's being bullied, excluded by people you thought were your friends, left out in group settings, or feeling like you're constantly fighting for basic needs in an unjust system, these experiences can leave lasting marks. They can shake our sense of safety and belonging and leave us feeling like we have to hide who we really are to fit in. No matter the cause, the path to healing usually starts with finding spaces where we're truly welcomed and valued.

One powerful way to do this is by joining communities that believe in your potential. The Acro community, for instance, is built on principles of inclusivity and support. Local Acro communities often have systems and shared values in place to make sure everyone feels seen and encouraged. Teachers and more experienced members often step into roles that foster growth. You'll likely find that they genuinely care about helping you learn and thrive. By connecting with these supportive leaders and role models, you may find people who not only see your potential, but actively help you nurture it. This kind of support can restore a sense of agency and help rebuild your trust in collective spaces.

One of the most beautiful aspects of Acro is that it replaces the competitive mindset, so common in sports and performance-based practices, with collaboration. Growth is celebrated communally. When one person learns a new skill, it tends to ripple out, encouraging others to try it too. Progress is shared, not hoarded, and support is mutual. Rather than comparing who's "better," people cheer each other on, creating a contagious sense of possibility and joy. This creates an environment where "failing forward" is encouraged. This supportive atmosphere helps us see that trying, messing up, and trying again are vital parts of growth, not something to be ashamed of.

This environment naturally cultivates **compersion**, the feeling of happiness for another's success. It's a radical shift from the scarcity-driven mindset that often underpins social and cultural systems. In Acro, someone else's growth doesn't diminish your own; it expands it. In Acro, you'll often see this in action as community members genuinely celebrate each other's breakthroughs. It's a refreshing shift from the competitive environments many of us grew up with, and it can help you redefine how you measure progress and success in your own life.

Finally, it's important to remember that our environment doesn't have to be defined by our past experiences. Even if you were born into an environment that didn't feel safe, welcoming, or supportive, you can choose to build or join communities that do. The culture of cooperation, emotional safety, and shared success in Acro offers an alternative to the disconnection many people feel from larger systems. It can provide reassurance that healing, growth, and belonging are possible, even after exclusion or invalidation.

When practiced with intention, Acro can become a powerful tool for emotional restoration, not just a physical discipline. The repeated experiences of co-regulation, mutual trust, and embodied communication offer a path to healing wounds that may have been carried for years. For many, these experiences begin to fill in gaps left by past relationships, or unmet emotional needs. They gently rewire the nervous system for connection, rather than protection. As your body learns that it's safe to be held, to fall and be caught, or to voice a need and have it respected, your internal landscape shifts, making space for more secure, resilient ways of relating.

Over time, incorporating Acro into your life can open doors to deeper fulfillment, not just within your partnerships, but in how you show up in the world. You may find yourself feeling more grounded, more connected to your body, and more open to vulnerability, joy, and authentic expression. The practice becomes a mirror and a coach, showing you where you still hold back, but also how far you've come. It reminds you that healing doesn't always look like therapy or stillness; sometimes, it looks like play, laughter, shared effort, and the courage to be seen. Through Acro, you can not only transform how you relate to others, but also how you relate to yourself.

Notes

1. *"Trust + Communication (w/ Lux Sternstein)," episode of Sorry to Podcast This, November 13, 2019.*
2. *Hübl and Avritt, "Toward the Integration of Collective Trauma."*

Bibliography

Ainsworth, Mary D. "The Development of Infant Mother Attachment." In Review of Child Development Research. Vol. 3, Child Development and Social Policy, edited by B. M. Caldwell and H. N. Ricciuti, 1–94. Chicago: University of Chicago Press, 1973.

Ainsworth, Mary D., Mary C. Blehar, Everett Waters, and Sally Wall. Patterns of Attachment: A Psychological Study of the Strange Situation. Hillsdale, NJ: Erlbaum, 1978.

Bakan, David. The Duality of Human Existence: An Essay on Psychology and Religion. Chicago: Rand McNally, 1966.

Baker, Levi R., Jennifer L. Luchies, and W. Keith Campbell. "Attachment and Jealousy: Understanding the Dynamic Experience of Jealousy via the Relationship Threat Appraisal Model." Personality and Social Psychology Bulletin 44, no. 12 (2018): 1664–80.

Balzarini, Rachel N., J. N. McDonald, Taylor Kohut, Justin J. Lehmiller, Brittany M. Holmes, and Jennifer J. Harman. "Compersion: When Jealousy-Inducing Situations Don't (Just) Induce Jealousy." Archives of Sexual Behavior 50, no. 4 (2021): 1311–24. https://doi.org/10.1007/s10508-020-01853-1.

Bartels, Andreas, and Semir Zeki. "The Neural Basis of Romantic Love." NeuroReport 11, no. 17 (2000): 3829–34.

Birnbaum, Gurit. "Attachment Orientations, Sexual Functioning, and Relationship Satisfaction in a Community Sample of Women." Journal of Social and Personal Relationships 24, no. 1 (2007): 21–35.

Birnbaum, Gurit E., Harry Reis, Mario Mikulincer, Omri Gillath, and Adi Orpaz. "When Sex Is More than Just Sex: Attachment Orientations, Sexual Experience, and Relationship Quality." Journal of Personality and Social Psychology 91, no. 5 (2006): 929–43.

Bowlby, John. Attachment and Loss. Vol. 1, Attachment. New York: Basic Books, 1969.

Bowlby, John. Attachment and Loss. Vol. 2, Separation: Anxiety and Anger. New York: Basic Books, 1973.

Brown, Brené. Dare to Lead: Brave Work. Tough Conversations. Whole Hearts. New York: Random House, 2018.

Brown, Brené, host. "Living BIG (Part 2 of 2 with A. B. Ruiz)." Episode of Unlocking Us. January 4, 2023. Vox Media. .

Brown, Daniel P., and David S. Elliott. Attachment Disturbances in Adults: Treatment for Comprehensive Repair. New York: W. W. Norton, 2016.

Buczynski, Ruth, course director. The Neurobiology of Attachment. Treating Trauma Master Series. Main Session no. 2. Professional course offered by the National Institute for the Clinical Application of Behavioral Medicine, 2019. https://www.nicabm.com/program/attachment/.

Butzer, Boris, and Lorne Campbell. "Adult Attachment, Sexual Satisfaction, and Relationship Satisfaction: A Study of Married Couples." Personal Relationships 15, no. 1 (2008): 141–54.

Campbell, Lorne, Jeffry A. Simpson, Jennifer Boldry, and David A. Kashy. "Perceptions of Conflict and Support in Romantic Relationships: The Role of Attachment Anxiety." Journal of Personality and Social Psychology 88, no. 3 (2005): 510–31.

Chapman, Gary D. The Five Love Languages: How to Express Heartfelt Commitment to Your Mate. Chicago: Northfield, 1995.

Collins, Nancy L., and Stephen J. Read. "Adult Attachment, Working Models, and Relationship Quality in Dating Couples." Journal of Personality and Social Psychology 58, no. 4 (1990): 644–63.

David, Shayna, Shlomo Hareli, and Ursula Hess. "The Influence on Perceptions of Truthfulness of the Emotional Expressions Shown When Talking about Failure." Europe's Journal of Psychology 11, no. 1 (2015): 125–38.

Earnshaw, Elizabeth. "Can You Defend Yourself Without Being Defensive? Here's How to Respond to Criticism the Right Way." mindbodygreen, November 27, 2019.

Fay, Deirdre. Becoming Safely Embodied: A Skills-Based Approach to Working with Trauma and Dissociation. n.p.: Heart Full Life, 2007.

Feeney, Judith A. "Adult Romantic Attachment: Developments in the Study of Couple Relationships." In Handbook of Attachment: Theory, Research, and Clinical Applications. 2nd ed., edited by Jude Cassidy and Phillip A. Shaver, 456–81. New York: Guilford Press, 2008.

Fern, Jessica. Polysecure: Attachment, Trauma and Consensual Nonmonogamy. Portland, OR: Thorntree Press, 2020.

Frazier, Patricia, Kelly Greer, Leslie A. Gabrielsen, Courtney Tennen, Annette M. Park, and John K. Tomich. "The Roles of Social Support in Recovery from Stress and Trauma." In The Oxford Handbook of Stress and Mental Health, edited by Kate L. Harkness and Elizabeth P. Hayden, 233–48. New York: Oxford University Press, 2020.

Frei, Jennifer R., and Phillip R. Shaver. "Respect in Close Relationships: Prototype Definition, Self-Report Assessment, and Initial Correlates." Personal Relationships 9, no. 2 (2002): 121–39.

Galtung, Johan. "Violence, Peace, and Peace Research." Journal of Peace Research 6, no. 3 (1969): 167–91.

Gottman Institute's Editorial Team. "What Is the Sound Relationship House?" Gottman.com, November 30, 2020. https://www.gottman.com/blog/what-is-the-sound-relationship-house/.

Gottman, John. The Science of Trust: Emotional Attunement for Couples. New York: W. W. Norton, 2011.

Gottman, John, and Joan DeClaire. The Relationship Cure: A 5 Step Guide to Strengthening Your Marriage, Family, and Friendships. New York: Three Rivers Press, 2001.

Gottman, John, Julie Schwartz Gottman, Doug Abrams, and Rachel Carlton Abrams. Eight Dates: Essential Conversations for a Lifetime of Love. New York: Workman, 2018.

Gottman, John, and Julie Schwartz Gottman. The Love Prescription. New York: Random House, 2022.

Gottman, John M. Marital Interaction: Empirical Investigations. New York: Academic Press, 1979.

Gottman, John M., James Coan, Sybil Carrére, and Catherine Swanson. "Predicting Marital Happiness and Stability from Newlywed Interactions." Journal of Marriage and the Family 60, no. 1 (1998): 5–22.

Gottman, John M., and Nan Silver. The Seven Principles for Making Marriage Work. New York: Three Rivers Press, 1999.

Gottman, John, and Nan Silver. Why Marriages Succeed or Fail: And How You Can Make Yours Last. New York: Simon & Schuster, 1994.

Gottman, Julie Schwartz, and John Gottman. Fight Right: How Successful Couples Turn Conflict into Connection. New York: Harmony Books, 2024.

Gross, James J. "Emotion Regulation: Affective, Cognitive, and Social Consequences." Psychophysiology 39, no. 3 (2002): 281–91.

Hamilton, Joli, Nicholas R. Morrison, and Ayla N. Gioia. "Jealousy: A Comparison of Monogamous and Consensually Non-Monogamous Women's Experience." Cogent Mental Health 3, no. 1 (2024). https://doi.org/10.1080/28324765.2023.22830.

Hanson, Rick. Hardwiring Happiness: The New Brain Science of Contentment, Calm, and Confidence. New York: Harmony Books, 2014.

Hazan, Cindy, and Phillip R. Shaver. "Romantic Love Conceptualized as an Attachment Process." Journal of Personality and Social Psychology 52, no. 3 (1987): 511–24.

Heller, Diane Poole. The Power of Attachment: How to Create Deep and Lasting Intimate Relationships. Boulder, CO: Sounds True, 2019.

Hepper, Ellen G., and Katherine B. Carnelley. "Attachment and Romantic Relationships: The Role of Models of Self and Other." In The Psychology of Love. Vol. 1, edited by Michele A. Paludi, 133–54. Santa Barbara, CA: Praeger, 2012.

Holland, D., and M. Arshad, hosts. "Trust + Communication (w/ Lux Sternstein)." Episode of I'm Sorry to Podcast This. November 13, 2019. Spotify.

Hübl, Thomas. "Attuned: Practicing Interdependence." Watkins Mind Body Spirit, Spring 2024, 77.

Hübl, Thomas, and Julie Jordan Avritt. "Toward the Integration of Collective Trauma in a Time of Exponential Change." Spanda Journal 7, no. 1 (2017): 75–84. https://spanda.org/assets/docs/spanda-journal-VII,1-2017.pdf.

Hübl, Thomas, and Lori Shridhare. "What Collective Trauma Feels Like." Psychology Today, March 5, 2025. https://www.psychologytoday.com/us/blog/attuned/202503/what-collective-trauma-feels-like.

Hussey, Matthew. "How to Know If You Should Keep Trying with Him." MatthewHussey.com, November 7, 2020. https://matthewhussey.com/blog/other/how-to-know-if-you-should-keep-trying-with-him/.

Joireman, Jeff, Tiffany L. Needham, and April L. Cummings. "Relationships between Dimensions of Attachment and Empathy." North American Journal of Psychology 4, no. 3 (2002): 63–80.

Joseph, Stephen. "Growth Following Adversity: Positive Psychological Perspectives on Posttraumatic Stress." Psihologijske Teme 18, no. 2 (2009): 335–44.

Kashdan, Todd B., Paul Rose, and Frank D. Fincham. "Curiosity and Exploration: Facilitating Positive Subjective Experiences and Personal Growth Opportunities." Journal of Personality Assessment 82, no. 3 (2004): 291–305. https://doi.org/10.1207/s15327752jpa8203_05.

Levenson, Robert W., and John M. Gottman. "Physiological and Affective Predictors of Change in Relationship Satisfaction." Journal of Personality and Social Psychology 49, no. 1 (1985): 85–94.

Levine, Amir, and Rachel Heller. Attached: Are You Anxious, Avoidant or Secure? How the Science of Adult Attachment Can Help You Find and Keep Love. London: Bluebird, 2019.

Main, Mary, and Judith Solomon. "Discovery of an Insecure-Disorganized/Disoriented Attachment Pattern." In Affective Development in Infancy, edited by M. Yogman and T. B. Brazelton, 95–124. Norwood, NJ: Ablex, 1986.

Mark, Kristen P., Lauren M. Vowels, and Sarah H. Murray. "The Impact of Attachment Style on Sexual Satisfaction and Sexual Desire in a Sexually Diverse Sample." Journal of Sex and Marital Therapy 44, no. 5 (2018): 450–58.

McCranie, Stephen. "Mastery." Doodle Alley Blog, January 10, 2010.

Mikulincer, Mario, Varda Florian, Philip A. Cowan, and Carolyn P. Cowan. "Attachment Security in Couple Relationships: A Systemic Model and Its Implications for Family Dynamics." Family Process 41, no. 3 (2002): 405–34.

Mikulincer, Mario, and Phillip R. Shaver. Attachment in Adulthood: Structure, Dynamics, and Change. 2nd ed. New York: Guilford Press, 2016.

Mogilski, Justin K., S. D. Reeve, S. C. A. Nicolas, S. H. Donaldson, V. E. Mitchell, and L. L. M. Welling. "Jealousy, Consent, and Compersion within Monogamous and Consensually Non-Monogamous Romantic Relationships." Archives of Sexual Behavior 48, no. 2 (2019): 1811–28. https://doi.org/10.1007/s10508-018-1286-4.

Moors, Amy C., William S. Ryan, and William J. Chopik. "Multiple Loves: The Effects of Attachment with Multiple Concurrent Romantic Partners on Relational Functioning." Personality and Individual Differences 147 (2019): 102–10. https://doi.org/10.1016/j.paid.2019.04.023.

Perel, Esther. Mating in Captivity. New York: HarperCollins, 2006.

Pogosyan, Marianna. "How We Help Each Other Heal: Much of Our Healing Can Take Place in Relation to Others." Psychology Today, April 4, 2024. https://www.psychologytoday.com/us/blog/between-cultures/202404/how-we-help-each-other-heal.

Primack, Brian A., Ariel Shensa, Jaime E. Sidani, Erin O. Whaite, Liu Yi Lin, Daniel Rosen, Jason B. Colditz, Ana Radovic, and Elizabeth Miller. "Social Media Use and Perceived Social Isolation among Young Adults in the U.S." American Journal of Preventive Medicine 53, no. 1 (2017): 1–8. https://doi.org/10.1016/j.amepre.2017.01.010.

Proyer, René T. "A New Structural Model for the Study of Adult Playfulness: Assessment and Exploration of an Understudied Individual Differences Variable." Personality and Individual Differences 108 (2017): 113–22.

Robbins, Tony. "#DateWithDestiny2025." Facebook video, December 5, 2025.

Rooney, Melanie. "Power & Consent in Acro." AcroYoga Austin, February 12, 2020. https://www.acroyogaaustin.org/power-and-consent.

Rosenberg, Marshall B. Nonviolent Communication: A Language of Life. Encinitas, CA: PuddleDancer Press, 2003.

Siegel, Daniel J. Mindsight: The New Science of Personal Transformation. New York: Bantam Books, 2010.

Simpson, Jeffry A., and Jay Belsky. "Attachment Theory within a Modern Evolutionary Framework." In Handbook of Attachment: Theory, Research, and Clinical Applications. 3rd ed., edited by Jude Cassidy and Phillip R. Shaver, 91–113. New York: Guilford Press, 2018.

Sinek, Simon. "Asking for Help Is an Act of Service." Video. Brilliant Minds Foundation, June 2024. LinkedIn. https://www.linkedin.com/posts/simonsinek_asking-for-help-is-an-act-of-service-don-activity-7230237373047975936-NRIK/.

Solomon, Alexandra H. Loving Bravely: 20 Lessons of Self-Discovery to Help You Get the Love You Want. Oakland, CA: New Harbinger, 2017.

Tatkin, Stan. We Do: Saying Yes to a Relationship of Depth, True Connection, and Enduring Love. Boulder, CO: Sounds True, 2019.

Tea and Consent. Video. Produced by Blue Seat Studios for Thames Valley Police and the Thames Valley Sexual Violence Prevention Group, 2015. YouTube.

Tedeschi, Richard G., and Lawrence G. Calhoun. "Posttraumatic Growth: Conceptual Foundations and Empirical Evidence." Psychological Inquiry 15, no. 1 (2004): 1–18.

Thomas, B. "A Brief History of Acroyoga: The Origin & Roots of Acrobatic Yoga." Slackrobats, July 19, 2017. https://slackrobats.com/acroyoga-history/.

Wallin, David J. Attachment in Psychotherapy. New York: Guilford Press, 2007.

Woodbury, Zhiwa. "Climate Trauma: Toward a New Taxonomy of Traumatology." Ecopsychology 11, no. 1 (2019): 1–8.

Zeifman, Debra, and Cindy Hazan. "Pair Bonds as Attachments: Reevaluating the Evidence." In Handbook of Attachment: Theory, Research, and Clinical Applications. 3rd ed., edited by Jude Cassidy and Phillip R. Shaver, 416–34. New York: Guilford Press, 2018.

About the Authors

Eric McKeethen

Eric McKeethen is an Acro teacher, performer, and community builder with more than a decade of experience in partner acrobatics and movement-based education. He has taught and performed with organizations including Pitch Catch Circus School, Acrobatic Conundrum, and Tempos Circus, and contributed to acro communities in Texas and Seattle. His background in marketing, leadership, and communications further informs his work, giving him a distinctive perspective on connection, trust, and the dynamics that shape strong partnerships.

Kate Burkett

Kate Burkett is a life coach, retreat leader, and AcroYoga practitioner with over a decade of experience fostering connection through movement, communication, and community. For more than fifteen years, she has led in-person and virtual gatherings for diverse audiences around the world, and she currently curates destination retreats centered on growth, adventure, and belonging. Through her coaching work focused on communication and self-respect, Kate has guided hundreds of clients toward more grounded, connected, and intentional relationships.

www.ingramcontent.com/pod-product-compliance
Lightning Source LLC
LaVergne TN
LVHW020703110826
845149LV00012B/2096
* 9 7 9 8 9 9 5 6 1 0 5 1 9 *